SPIT ONCE FOR LUCK

Fostering Julie, a disturbed child

SPIT ONCE FOR LUCK

Fostering Julie, a disturbed child

JOHN SWAIN

Foreword by Dr Jean S. Heywood
Lecturer, Faculty of Economics and
Social Studies, University of Manchester

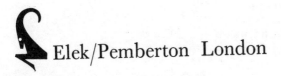

Elek/Pemberton London

To Jade, Anna and, of course, Julie

First published in Great Britain in 1977
by Elek Books Ltd
54—58 Caledonian Road, London N1 9RN
in association with
Pemberton Publishing Co. Ltd.

ISBN 0 236 40091 6

Printed in Great Britain by
Biddles Limited, Guildford, Surrey

Acknowledgements

I am grateful to Brian, Madeline and Penny for writing down their experiences with Julie for me.

NOTE

In accordance with the wishes of the social services the identity of all the institutions and individuals connected with the institutions mentioned in this book have been disguised so that no one will know the true identity of Julie.

Foreword

From time to time we are privileged to read the autobiographies of adults who have spent their childhood in care, and researchers have published biographical anthologies of children who have been adopted or fostered. These usually are the expressions of very articulate individuals. By the nature of things those who have been grossly damaged, both emotionally and educationally, by childhood deprivation have found no way of putting their feelings into a form acceptable for publication; it is not easy, therefore, for us to know them from the inside. All the more exciting then, to come across this book, an account written by a sensitive, knowledgeable foster-father of the situation of such a deprived child, one almost abandoned by the educational and social services as too damaged to help. Almost, but not quite, and, clearly, what saved Julie was the educational service for the mentally handicapped and the ability of one of its teachers, John Swain, and his wife, to enter into the mind and feelings of an unhappy child and offer in their own home the love and caring, based on understanding, essential for the development of human dignity. The sacrificial quality of this love is apparent as we read the book, and it underlines the reason why fostering is perhaps the only way in which such a damaged child can be reassured, by actual experience, of the care, understanding and security which does exist in the world. It seems that the very stresses within the nuclear family — authority and rebellion, despair and hope, independence and possessive love — generate trust and self-confidence as they are overcome. The support at crucial times of two sets of grand parents and of real friends extends that atmosphere of trust.

There are lessons in this book for the services involved, but also for the wider community of concerned men and women. The work which has been successful with Julie cannot be done by isolated foster parents, or in the course of a professional task with fixed hours of work, however much the professionalism is disguised. Support and recognition needs to be given by all of us to those who undertake such fostering as Julie is receiving. We are fortunate indeed to have such foster parents as Mr and Mrs Swain.

Jean S Heywood
Reader in Social Administration
March 1977   *University of Manchester*

Chapter 1

As I walked into the headmistress's office a small, skinny child looked up at me. She was dressed in an ill-fitting cat-suit, stretched bright red jumper and a pair of old suede shoes. She was as stooped and emaciated as a crone. Her face was thin and white and she had dark rings around her flashing frightened eyes. There was more than fear in her eyes though; there was so much hatred that she looked almost evil. There was certainly nothing very child-like about her.

She was spitting, but not in a way that I had seen anyone spit before. The spit flew from her mouth in what amounted to a continuous stream, landing about a foot from her shoes. Her mouth threw out spit mechanically, with the same unconscious ease with which other people swallow. One felt that if she were to stand in the same spot for very long a large pool would form rather like Alice's pool of tears in *Alice in Wonderland*. She was also masturbating. Her back was bent and one leg was slightly raised to enable her to keep one hand between her legs.

'This is Julie Lincoln,' said the nurse who was holding her hand.

'Hello Julie,' I said.

'Hello.' (spit) 'What your name?' (spit, spit) Her speech was surprisingly clear.

'I'm John,' I answered. 'Does she do that all the time?' I asked, turning to the nurse.

'Yes, she does. She never stops spitting or masturbating.' There was a note of repugnance in her voice.

'Want Penny,' said Julie.

'Go with John,' said the headmistress. 'He'll look after you.'

'How long is she here for?' I asked her.

'She may only be here for a few weeks,' she answered. 'You'd better take her down to the gym now.'

I could see that she was getting a little anxious about her office carpet, so I took Julie's hand and led her towards the door. Her hand was artistically long and thin and it was as cold and clammy as a dead fish.

'Good luck,' said the nurse and Julie and I walked out of the office into the warm sunshine of August 1974. I was a teacher in the school attached to a hospital for the mentally handicapped, and Julie was my new pupil. As she walked along beside me, spitting and masturbating, we talked. This was a novelty to me as most of the children at the school had no speech at all, and none could speak as well as Julie.

'Want see Doulga',' she said.

'Who's Douglas?'

'Oh, Dougla'. Wheelchair,' she said as if she were reminding me of someone I should have known.

'Did you used to know him where you came from?'

'Di'.'

'You'll probably see him again then,' I said. 'Why do you spit, Julie?'

'Bad habit,' she replied. 'Shoes hur'.'

'Why? Are they too small?'

'It i'.'

She stopped. Her eyes were glazed and her face contorted with some private anguish.

'Want Penny,' she said.

'Where's Penny?' I asked.

'Schoo'.'

'What's the name of the school?'

'Oh, Rose Hill.' She was reminding me again.

'Was Penny your teacher there?' I asked.

'It i',' she replied.

We stepped over Jeremy A. who sat in the doorway of the gym totally engrossed with a sock he was flicking from side to side. Jeremy did little else other than flick socks or endlessly spin objects into the air. He could spin and catch a ball with the skill of a juggler. He spoke only when he was very excited or upset and then he would say, 'Oooo ya bugger, ya mucky bugger.'

10

We walked into the gym.

'Don't like it,' said Julie. 'Don't like gym.'

'Come on. Come on in and see the other children.'

'Want Penny,' she moaned.

In the gym that morning were most of the school, staff and children. My class of younger children was there: Sally and Norman running around; Maureen and Norah wandering around, lost in their own little worlds; Mick in his wheelchair. The older boys were there too. Smithy, 'big fat Smithy', the boy who could eat endlessly and who occasionally relieved his frustration by smashing windows, was on the rope swing. Harold stood silent and sinister over by the wall-bars. He was a strange boy who would obey every command to the letter and rarely did anything spontaneously, except when in a violent mood. In such moods he would suddenly let out a piercing scream and start gnawing at his wrist which was scarred with teeth marks. His strength was incredible; once he smashed the top of a porcelain toilet with one blow. Joe, the boy with a huge imagination and the ability to experience ecstasy from things most people ignore, was screeching with delight as he hung from the topmost wall-bar and let a handful of beer-mats float to the floor. Sligo and John were playing the record player. Finally, there were the 'low grades', a number of adolescent boys, rocking and salivating, waiting to be 'potted' (taken to the toilet).

'Not keen,' moaned Julie.

'OK', I said. 'Perhaps we could go for a walk.'

I took her over to meet Neil, one of the teachers. I had to drag Julie across the gym. She was screeching: 'Don't like it'; 'Not keen'; 'Gym smell'; 'Want Penny.' Neil grinned at her.

'Know how you feel,' he said to her. 'Does she do that all the time?' Neil asked watching Julie's spitting in amazement.

'Seems so. Her name's Julie and she isn't feeling so pleased at the moment, as you can hear.'

'What's up Julie? This place enough to make you spit, eh?'

'Want walk.' Julie was almost screaming.

'I think I had better take her for a walk,' I said. 'It must all be a bit strange for her.'

'Right. See you back at school then. We'll get the others back for you. See you, Julie,' he said.

11

Julie calmed as we walked back out into the sunshine.

'Nice day today isn't it, Julie?' I said.

'Who nice day for?' she asked.

'I mean the sun's shining and it's warm.'

'It i',' she said. 'Who John two name?'

'You want to know my second name?'

'It i'.'

'John Swain.'

'Who John Swain for?'

'I don't know what you mean, Julie.'

She changed the subject. 'Julie walk on wall?' she asked.

'All right then.'

She coped easily on the wall, and still managed to keep masturbating.

'Where did you live before you came here?'

'Oh, hostel.'

'Do you know when you are going back?'

'September. How long it i'?'

'A few weeks,' I said. 'Anyway let's go back to the school now.'

I held her as she clambered down. Spit flew all around but none went on me. She had perfect aim. When we reached the classroom the trouble started again. She began to whine, 'Don't like dis room.' 'Don't like John.' 'Want Penny.' I left her to it and turned my attention to the other children.

Two confrontations took place that morning which left me at a loss as to how I was to handle Julie. First there was her refusal to go to the toilet.

'Want toilet,' she said soon after we got in from the walk.

'OK, June will take you.' (June was a teaching assistant. She helped me around the classroom.) June took Julie off to the toilet but returned a minute later looking a little upset. She explained that when they had reached the toilet Julie had started screaming that she had already been, and she had kicked June on the shin.

'I don't know whether I'm going to like this little girl,' said June who was usually the most tolerant of people.

'Don't like June,' said Julie with conviction.

I continued to play with Norman and a couple of minutes later Julie again said, 'Want toilet.'

'Do you really want to go this time?' I said.

'Do.'

'Right. Then I'll take you, but I'm not playing about with you. Do you hear?'

'It i'.'

When we reached the door of the toilet Julie became agitated.

'No. Just been. Just been,' she protested.

'No, you haven't just been at all.'

'Been,' she screamed again.

I tried to pull her through the door but she would not move. She screamed and cried. She was terrified of going into the toilet.

'All right, all right,' I said softly. 'Just come and sit on the toilet and try.'

'Don't want to go.'

I gave up and took her back to the classroom. Two minutes later she repeated her demand to be taken to the toilet. I took her to the toilet three times that morning but got the same response each time. When I refused to take her to the toilet again she started to moan: 'Will go now'; 'Weeing myself'; 'It's coming now'; 'Julie dirty.' Two other teachers took pity on her and took her to the toilet, but they got the same response as myself.

The second confrontation involved kicking. While I was attempting to get Julie to join in playing with Norman she kicked him. I slapped her legs, not hard, but enough to let her know that she must control herself. She was shocked and spoke indignantly.

'John hur' me. Don't like John.'

I shrugged. 'If you kick someone, you expect to get hurt back,' I said and continued to play with Norman.

'Piss off,' said Julie.

It was obvious that Julie's isolation in the classroom was going to be a difficult problem.

Dinner time came and I left for my break. I decided that I would work with Julie that afternoon to try to stop her spitting. Before Julie had come to the hospital I had had a little girl called Rose in my class. Rose had screaming tantrums at the slightest frustration. These had been dealt

13

with in two ways: by slapping her to try to bring her round, but this invariably made her worse; or by isolating her until she calmed down, but this did not help either. I tried to put myself between Rose and her frustration. This in effect meant that I held Rose whenever she went into a tantrum. She would scream, try to hit me, kick me, hammer me with her head, and even bite me. I would hold on, trying to see that neither Rose nor myself were hurt, until her temper subsided in a flood of tears. Within weeks Rose's tantrums were fewer in number and far less severe, and the way was open to do other work with her. I had seen teachers deal with unacceptable behaviour in the same way that I dealt with Rose's tantrums and it almost invariably helped. My hope was that I could help Julie by holding her until she stopped spitting.

It had turned into one of the warmest afternoons of that summer. A number of children had already wandered out into the yard which passed for a playground at the school. I found Julie in the porch on her own, spitting and masturbating.

'Hello, Julie,' I said.

'Hello, where been?'

'I've been out. Would you like to come into the yard with me this afternoon?'

'Do.'

'Well just wait here. I'll be with you in a minute.'

I found June in the classroom. I told her that I meant to spend the rest of the day with Julie and asked her to look after the class. I picked up a couple of chairs, collected Julie and we went into the yard. She knelt on her chair and I sat beside her.

'Well, Julie, tell me why you spit.'

'Bad habit,' she replied.

'You could swallow like everyone else.'

'Can't. Spit got germs.'

'That's silly.'

'Mi' Cartwrigh' said it.'

'I don't know who she is but that is rubbish. Listen Julie, spit hasn't got germs.'

'It i'.'

'Am I swallowing germs then?' I asked.

'Germs make you poorly?' she responded.

Julie had the idea that saliva contained germs and try as I might I could not persuade her otherwise. After a while I changed my tactics.

'Would you like to go on a bus to the big town down the hill there? I could take you if you stopped spitting.'

'See Penny?' she asked becoming interested.

'Yes, if we can.'

'On train?'

'I'll take you on the train to Penny when you stop spitting. I can't take you if you're spitting you know. There's a sign which says "No Spitting" on the train.'

'Want train.'

'Well, I'll help you stop spitting then.' I told her.

'Can't. Handicap'. Spit got germs.'

'Rubbish,' I said, 'I'll help you to stop,' and as I spoke I put my arm around her; tilting her head back, I tried to hold her lips together. Julie cried out and tried to prise my hands open.

'Let go,' she squealed. 'Bad habit. Can't.' Spit was flying around everywhere and as she repeated each phrase her voice reached screaming pitch.

'No, I won't let go,' I retorted. 'Not until you stop spitting.'

Eventually I managed to close her lips and stop the stream of spit. Her eyes were large with terror and hatred. Tears poured down her cheeks. I held her, getting my breath back.

'If I let go will you spit?' She shook her head. 'If you do I'll get hold of you again straight away. Do you hear?'

She nodded. I let go and a large mess of spit shot out from her mouth, followed by several smaller amounts. Again we fought, Julie screeching and desperately trying to push me away while I tried to get hold of her mouth. All the time I spoke gently to her, telling her that habits could be broken and that spit had no germs. Four of five times more I managed to get hold of her mouth but each time I let go Julie spat. Then I had another idea. I got hold of her again and shouted to Carol, who was one of the more capable children. She had been watching the pantomime between Julie and myself in bewildered amusement. I sent her for a cup of water.

'Right, when Carol returns with the water we are going to wash the spit down,' I told Julie. She shook her head, as far as she could with me holding her mouth.

'Oh yes, we are. You want to go on buses and trains with us, don't you? I might even be able to take you to see Penny.' This time Julie nodded.

Carol returned with the water.

'When I let go of Julie's mouth put the cup to her lips and let her have a drink of water. Do you understand Carol?'

Carol nodded. I released Julie, she spat and Carol doused her with water. Julie shrieked with indignation.

A minute later I had stopped the flow of spit again, Carol had brought more water and we were ready for another attempt. The second, third and fourth attempts with the water were much the same as the first. Carol was managing to pour less water but Julie always managed to spit and close her lips before the water reached her mouth. Although we had had no success, Julie was becoming calmer and fighting less.

'This time I'm going to open your mouth for you,' I told her. She grunted her disapproval and shook her head, but it seemed to be the only way. I prised open Julie's mouth and Carol carefully poured the water in. Julie swallowed.

'It's gone?' I asked, releasing her.

'Gone,' said Julie. Her eyes were alight with pleasure and surprise, but then she spat again. I immediately got hold of her and we went through the same process.

'It's gone?' I asked again.

She nodded.

'If I let you go will you spit again?'

She shook her head. I gently eased my grip on her. She knelt there, no longer yelling or even moaning and no longer spitting.

'Is your mouth full again?' I asked.

'It i'.'

I gave her the cup of water and she took a sip and swallowed.

'Whenever it's full,' I said, 'take a sip of water. All right?'

'See Penny?'

'I'll have to find out where Penny is.'

'Go on train?'

'Yes, of course you can.'

'Not spitting now.'

'No you're not.' I said.

It had taken nearly two hours. She did spit again but the incessant spitting had stopped. She was no longer masturbating either. She had needed two hands to fend me off and, without either of us realising it, she had stopped masturbating.

It was four o'clock and time for Julie to return to the ward. A nurse arrived to escort her back and Julie took her hand without question. She was no more than two steps from me before she started spitting and masturbating again.

'See,' she said in a matter-of-fact voice. 'Spitting now.'

Some time later I learnt that Julie had been spitting and masturbating almost continuously for about five years before she arrived at the hospital.

Chapter 2

Next morning as Julie entered the classroom I raised her chin and she stopped spitting.

'What about your hand?' I asked.

She looked at it and then thrust it more firmly into her crutch.

'Where you been?' she asked.

'Move that hand before I smack you,' I said and she pulled her hand away. The saliva was building up in her mouth, so I gave her a sip of water from a paper cup which I had ready.

'Not dat cup,' she said.

'What?'

'Oh, blue,' she reminded me.

'You mean we used the blue cup last time?'

'It i'.'

'Well we'll have to use this cup today.'

'No. Want blue,' she shrieked.

'I don't know where it is,' I said, 'so you'll have to use this one.'

Her eyes flickered around the classroom.

'Oh, der ti',' she said pointing to the top of the cupboard. The cup was there, all but hidden by my coat.

'So it is,' I said reaching for it. I swopped the water over and gave her another swallow of water.

Julie had changed from spitting to 'swallowing for John', as she put it. Each morning as she came into the classroom I would raise her chin and the spitting would be contained. It was like switching off a machine. She would then begin to fill her mouth with saliva and I had to make her get rid of it each time. This would happen at least a hundred times a day. She absolutely refused to 'swallow for' anyone else and started spitting whenever I left her and sometimes even spat when I turned my back to her. As she left to return to the ward each evening after school the spitting and masturbating would begin again.

This filling of her mouth with saliva bemused me. I tried filling my mouth by not swallowing, to gain some appreciation of what it felt like. It is a difficult and very uncomfortable thing to do, requiring determination. I found that I swallowed every time my mind wandered. Yet Julie did it with ease. She never forgot to retain the saliva. I felt that either there was something yogi-like about her ability to control her body or there was something physically wrong which caused her difficulties with her swallowing. I saw Dr C, the consultant psychiatrist attached to the hospital, and asked him about this problem. His opinion was that Julie had no physical impediment, and it was entirely a behavioural problem.

'See Penny,' she demanded.

'Not today, but we are going out on a train, just as I promised. Do you want to go on a train?'

'It i'.' Shoes hurt,' she moaned.

'Are they too small?'

'It i'.'

'Well there's nothing I can do about that I'm afraid.'

'Wrong fee',' she said.

'No they're not on the wrong feet.'

'Want wrong fee'.' Her voice was becoming peevish.

'What for? They'll only hurt even more.'

'Want wrong fee'.' Her voice reached a high-pitched whine.

'Put them on the wrong feet then,' I said.

'Can't. Julie handicap'. John do,' she demanded.

'All right then,' I said giving in, 'sit down and I'll do it.'

As I bent down she asked,

'Who wrong fee' for?'

'I don't know. You asked me.'

'It i'.'

'This is a bit silly, isn't it?' I asked, looking up at her.

'Want wrong fee',' she screamed and I complied to please her.

'Tighter,' she said as I finished.

'But that's as tight as they'll go.'

'Too slack.'

I just shrugged.

'Laces too long,' she said.

'Look, do you want to go out or not?'

'Might twip up.'

'All right then,' I said, and tucked her laces in. 'Are your shoes all right now?'

She stood and rocked back and forth on her heels.

'Shoes too tigh'.' she moaned.

'Do you want to go or not?' I said a little louder.

During those first two weeks of having Julie at school I learnt just how awkward and obstinate one child could be. She demanded my absolute and complete attention and made it very difficult for me to give the other children in the class their due attention. She would scream and sometimes spit when I even talked to anyone else. She clung to me like a baby monkey most of the time, and chattered like one too. At the slightest rejection from me she would retreat to the wall looking thoroughly dejected. She showed little interest in any of the usual class activities or educational equipment. She refused to be part of the class or play with the other children, and only ever really showed any positive response when I took her for walks. Yet even on these walks she tended to be miserable and uncooperative.

'Too col',' said Julie as I helped her into her coat.

'Outside you mean?' I asked.

'It i'.'

'But it's a lovely sunny day.'

'What for?'

'Well because it's summer, I suppose. Look you've been nagging all day for a walk,' I said.

'Too windy,' she moaned.

'What's wrong with you? Do you or don't you want to go for a walk?'

'Do want walk,' she said.

'Well come on, let's go.'

Just as I opened the door Julie spat. I shut the door and looked at her.

'Will swallow now,' she pleaded looking at me in dread.

'I told you I wouldn't take you out if you were spitting.'

20

'Not spitting now.'

Eventually I agreed to take her, hoping that she would cheer up a little outside. As we ran down the hill for the bus I stumbled and all the water in the cup spilt on the pavement.

'Who fall for?' Julie asked, smiling for once.

'I tripped,' I replied.

'Why?'

'We were running too fast and my foot slipped off the curb.'

I showed her the empty cup.

'What shall we do now?' I asked, a little apprehensively.

'Oh, pretend dwink,' said Julie, as if it were obvious. She was still smiling.

'Pretend drink? Show me.'

Julie took the cup and put it to her lips. She pulled my hand to the cup, and when I pushed the cup to her mouth she swallowed.

'See,' she said, and that was the beginning of the 'swallowing-cup' method of making Julie swallow. We were to carry that 'swallowing cup' everywhere during the next four weeks, pushing it to her mouth every few minutes.

It was this sort of unpredictability in Julie's behaviour which daily increased my interest in her.

Julie chattered constantly, even through mouthfuls of saliva. From the first, it was this ability to hold a conversation, ask questions, and remember details which made her stand out from the rest of the children in the school. Her two favourite subjects were footwear and bodily functions. She was always inspecting people's shoes to see whether 'heels doin' down', and always knew when anyone had changed their footwear. Her conversations about shoes had a monotonous obsessiveness about them. Her conversations about 'bodily functions' however were not quite so bad and her strings of probing questions took us quite deep into physiology.

'Who need bloo' for?' Julie would ask.

'You need blood to carry oxygen around your body,' I said.

'Talk 'bout bloo'.'

Then her interrogation would begin: 'What made of?'

21

'Why?' 'You have no red bloo' cells . . . .?' 'Who need oxygen for?' 'Where air come from?' 'You have no air?' As I answered each question as well as I could, she would come up with a further one. There was never a satisfactory conclusion to these conversations. She never tired of asking questions and the only way of ending these talks was for me to refuse to answer. It was in this way, though, that I found out about Julie's surprising vocabulary and her ability to learn new words. Even words such as 'haemoglobin' would be recalled by her the next day.

Julie was a total enigma to me. The more I learnt about her the more of a puzzle she became. She seemed to be backward but so disturbed that it was difficult to tell how intelligent she really was Her behaviour was, to say the least, highly unusual, but it was not at all the behaviour of a severely subnormal child. It was true that many of the types of problems she revealed were the same as those of the other children, yet the extent and exact nature of the problems themselves were very different. Some of the children in the school masturbated occasionally; Julie, on the other hand, masturbated all the time, apart from when she was with me. Some of the children slavered; Julie spat. Many of the children were doubly incontinent; Julie refused to go to the toilet. Many of the children had difficulty feeding themselves; Julie refused to eat. As for how to deal with her, I was really working in the dark. Training Julie was very different from training the other children in the class. Toilet training a severely subnormal child is a slow and methodical business. The 'toilet training' of Julie just happened one morning.

'Want toilet,' said Julie and gave me a look of pure hatred. My heart sank. We were about to embark on a trip to town and needed to hurry for the bus.

'Well I'm not taking you. I've taken you a dozen times and all you do when you get there is start screaming,' I said.

'No. Will wee dis time.'

'I don't believe you.'

'Wee wee coming now.'

'If I take you to that toilet and you don't do anything I'm not taking you out,' I told her. 'Now do you still want to go?'

'It i',' she insisted.

'Who Julie go toilet for?' she asked as we walked into the lavatory. She faltered but I pulled her in. She was petrified but, as yet, she was not screaming.

'I don't know.'

'Bladder full,' she told me.

I undid her cat-suit for her. Again she hesitated so I pressed her down until she was sitting on the toilet.

'Won't come,' she said immediately.

'But you haven't tried yet.'

She started to stand but I pushed her down again.

'Can't wee. Handicap'.' She was crying now.

'You want to go out don't you?'

'It i'.'

'Well try to wee Julie. Now,' I shouted.

'Press tummy?' she asked.

'I suppose so,' I answered, not understanding what she meant.

She began to dig her fingers deep into her abdomen. She was still agitated and yet her attitude seemed to have changed.

'John do it,' she said. Her voice had an edge of hysteria.

'What? Press your tummy?'

'It i'.'

I leaned over her. She took my hands and she pressed my fingers into her abdomen as hard as she could. Suddenly she relieved herself. She looked up and grinned as it came flooding out. She must have been absolutely desperate to go. She seemed to be trying to press every last drop she could from her bladder.

'Who wee wee for?' she asked.

'Because your bladder was full.'

'Who need it for?'

'What?' I asked.

'Bladder. Talk 'bout bladder,' she said, leading into another conversation.

The most worrying aspect of this so-called training, apart from the fact that she frequently reverted and refused to go to the toilet, was that it was specific to myself. As with the

23

swallowing. Julie would 'wee wee for John' and she did i
for nobody else but myself. The only thing I could do
however, was to try to work on the relationship between us
hoping that it would, in time, help her to relate to others

Chapter 3

During her third week at school Julie and I, together with a small group of children and staff, went to camp for five days. The camp consisted of three wooden huts in the grounds of another hospital which was out in the countryside near a Northern market town. This put us in a different situation.

On the first night at camp I saw Julie in a new light. Her constant prattling and rapid, seemingly reasonless, changes of mood during the journey to the camp had been wearing. She had refused to eat and only performed on the lavatory when I threatened to leave her out all night. This Julie I knew already, but at bedtime I saw a far more pathetic girl. Firstly, I saw her without clothes. Her arms and legs were shockingly thin and shapeless. Her abdomen looked swollen and her ribs could have been counted. Her back was humped rather than just bent. Her physique reminded me of those pictures of children in areas of famine. I believe that she weighed around two stone at that time, though she was almost twelve years old. Later that night I saw her in bed. At first I thought that she was not there. The night was warm and most of the children were sprawled in their beds. Fatty Smithy had pushed off all his covers and lay there naked. Yet Julie's bed was hardly disturbed. Eventually I realized that she was sleeping curled up on her knees at the bottom of it. The lump was so small that it was hard to believe there was a child in the bed at all. I lifted the covers and found that they smelt and were soaked in spit. I had disturbed her and she moved in her sleep and spat. She seemed pitifully lost. Pity was not one of the feelings Julie usually aroused.

One problem with Julie that had to be faced at camp was her refusal to eat. I had seen severely subnormal children who grossly overate and severely subnormal children who would grovel about the floor and eat absolutely anything left lying around, but this was the first child I had dealt with who refused to eat at all. Eating, for most children, is a time of relaxation and ease. Food, particularly sweets, are used as rewards. It is the one thing that can be relied upon to get a positive response. Julie had reversed this more usual behaviour. Food always produced a negative response and eating for her was a time of tension and fight.

To help me deal with this problem I had been given a number of packets of Julie's 'special diet' by the hospital. This was to be mixed with water to form a liquid which contained all the correct nutrients, in the correct proportions. Its taste was 'natural'. This diet was costing around four pounds a go. This solution to the problem involved an acceptance of Julie's behaviour and its purpose was to alleviate the consequences of her refusal to eat. I had, however, heard of a different method of tackling the problem. I had attended a lecture by a lady who ran a home for autistic children, and she had told of a boy she had dealt with who would eat only food which had been mashed to a pulp. At the home they had tackled the problem by not accepting his behaviour and by forcing the boy to eat the same food as the other children. She told of the first nightmare meals when two or three staff would have to hold the boy while she fed him. Within four months he was eating absolutely normally and was well on the road to overcoming his other problems. Such an approach was similar to the one I had already used with Julie to stop her spitting, and seemed to be one that might help her overcome her eating problem.

On the second day at camp I took it easy with the eating problem. I tried the special diet. 'It's horrible,' said Julie. I tasted it and could only agree with her. I produced breakfast cereal, soup and bread, and rice pudding; trying to persuade her to eat. These opening gambits were a failure. I did, however, discover her battery of reasons as to why she should not eat or drink: 'Too har'; 'Too ho'; 'Too col'; 'It's lumpy' (even the soup was lumpy); 'Got germs'; and simply 'Don't like i'.' These 'reasons' became quite bizarre at times: 'Milk make you thirsty'; 'Chicken gi' thin legs'; and even 'Shandy make hairs on fanny'. When she sat to eat her eyes would flit around and the blood completely drain from her face. She would hunch her back and freeze.

On the third day I made my first determined attempt to feed Julie. We sat down together in front of a plate of steak and kidney pie, mashed potatoes and peas. Julie looked at it with revulsion.

'Don't like i',' she said.

I helped myself to a spoonful of potato.

'Delicious,' I said.

'Don't like mea',' she whined.

'Well you're going to eat something,' I answered trying to sound confident.

'No. Too har' for Julie.'

'Let's try some mashed potato first. It's lovely and soft.'

I got a spoonful of potato and held it out to her.

'No,' she screeched and knocked my arm away.

'Yes,' I said grabbing hold of her hands, but as I pushed the spoon towards her, her head twisted away.

'Too lumpy,' she cried.

'Rubbish,' I retorted.

I rearranged my attacking position. I held her hands between my legs, and was then able to twist her head back, prise her mouth open and push in the potato. I let go of her head and she spat it out. I repeated the process but this time I did not let her go. I picked up her 'swallowing cup' and pushed it to her mouth.

'Water,' she managed to say.

'You mean you'll swallow it if I get you some water?'

She nodded.

One of the other teachers brought me a cup of water, but by then she had struggled free and had spat out the food. Again I repeated the process; however this time I managed to pour a little water between her clamped lips and she swallowed before I released her.

'See,' she said.

'That was all right wasn't it?' I asked.

'Full,' she said.

In this way, though she did spit out a great deal of the food, I managed to get her to eat most of the meal. From then on at camp, Julie ate the same food as the other children. With each successive meal the battle became slightly less fierce, but I had to sit over her at all times ready to use force; otherwise the food was spat out. Each meal took anything up to a full hour.

At camp I learnt more about Julie's extremes of mood. At times she would become unconsolably depressed and withdrawn, while at other times she would completely lose her self-control and become hysterical. The worst of these occasions was when we went on a conducted tour of an underground cave. She became anxious as soon as we entered the cave.

'Don't like it,' she said.

The corridor of the cave was rather cold and a little claustrophobic so I tried to take her back out.

'No,' she screamed. 'Want cave.'

'All right, all right,' I said and we carried on into the cave.

The party stopped while the guide tried to explain the history of the cave to our children, none of whom could understand what she was saying.

'Too col',' Julie moaned.

'Ssh.'

'Won't,' she yelled. 'Don't like cave.'

'Listen to the lady, Julie.'

'Don't like lady.' She was crying and rocking nervously.

'Please, Julie,' I pleaded.

'Don't like John.'

'Hush.'

'Piss off,' she screamed and the words echoed down the cave.

'Is the little girl all right?' asked the guide, who could hardly be heard above Julie's screeching.

'Yes, thank you. She'll be all right soon,' I answered putting my hand over Julie's mouth.

We moved on further into the cave and Julie's eruption calmed to a low grumbling: 'Don't like knickers'; 'No tea tonight'. Eventually we reached an underground river at the heart of the cave and again the party stopped for the guide to give her talk. At this point Julie lost all control. She spat, she screamed, and she threw her vital 'swallowing cup' into the water. I tried to hold her but she was kicking and lashing out wildly. The guide moved quickly on. Julie was like a spitting wildcat. I had almost no room to restrain her in the confines of the cave and my only option was to usher her out as quickly as possible. It was only when we emerged into the fresh air again that she calmed down.

We sat together on a wall recovering. She had stopped spitting and her mouth was filling with saliva.

'Well you lost your cup.' I said.

'New one,' she suggested.

'There's nowhere round here we can get one. Look, just get rid of it,' I said and pushed her mouth with my hand. She swallowed and we both laughed with relief.

'Where blue cup now?' she asked.

'Somewhere in the middle of the river,' I answered.

As well as the periods of fighting and the difficulty of coping with Julie, there were a number of happier periods at camp. There was, for instance, the day we went shopping for a pair of new boots.

'Who needs new boots for?' she asked.

'Well, these are old and you say they hurt.'

'Throw ol' ones away?'

'No, we'll keep those for going in puddles.'

'Who ol' shoes hur' for?'

'I don't know,' I replied.

'Oh, too ti'. Who too ti' for?'

'You tell me.'

'Oh, feet drown,' she answered.

She ran excitedly to a shoeshop window and she pressed her nose against the glass.

'Ooo, like dese,' she said.

'Those are ladies' shoes. They've got high heels.'

'Who high heels for?'

'To make you tall,' I replied.

'Ooo, like tall.'

'No, Julie, come and look at these children's shoes. Look, there are some baseball boots there. You like baseball boots.'

'Where?' she asked.

'There.'

'Baseball boo'. Baseball boo',' she squealed in excitement.

'Which colour do you want?'

29

'Orange.'

'They've only got blue and red.'

She settled for blue, and we went into the shop. Julie rushed around shrieking with delight. She grabbed the feet of a very startled shop assistant, who happened to be wearing a curious pair of orange high heels, and nearly upended her. I managed to calm her and we set about trying on baseball boots.

'Want wrong fee,' she said.

'Do you want these boots or not, Julie?' I asked.

'Want high heels.'

'It's baseball boots or nothing at all. Now let me put them on the right feet, or I'm going to take you out and there'll be no boots at all.'

Julie looked at the boots when I had finally put them on her. She grinned.

'Do you like them?'

'It i'.' She examined them. 'Heels doin' down?'

'No, the heels are not going down.'

'Want high heels,' she moaned as we left the shop.

She was so proud of her new boots that in the Post Office she lifted her foot on to the counter to show the assistant.

'Look, new boo',' she said triumphantly.

'Yes, dear,' answered the assistant.

On the whole Julie improved during those five days at camp. She still clung to me, desperately demanding attention, and still had to use the 'swallowing cup' (we had bought a new one) every other minute. It was still difficult to get her to eat and use the toilet. Yet all the fights with her were becoming easier, and her misery was tempered by many more smiles.

While driving back to the hospital, Julie cried. It was the first time that I had ever seen her cry because she was sad rather than because she was upset. She just cried quietly and pleaded not to be taken back to the hospital. I led her into the ward and handed her over to a nurse.

'Oh no, not dis adain,' said Julie. Tears rolled down her cheeks as the spit started to fly from her mouth.

The week that followed camp was dreadful. Julie lost all the progress that she had made during camp. She started to

30

spit when I was with her several times and I had to go through the whole process of holding her again. Her total misery was a marked contrast to her attitude at camp. However, there were two changes in the situation at school which made me more determined to help her. First, I had decided to leave and had started to apply for jobs elsewhere. I wanted to see some change for the better in Julie before I left. Secondly, a small class of difficult children, including Julie, had been formed for a more intensive type of treatment. I was to be one of the three teachers dealing with this class. This enabled me to devote more time to Julie without neglecting other children.

Chapter 4

During the time that I have known Julie I have found out enough about her life before I met her to be able piece together most of her history. This, together with her own telling of the story, helped me to get a better understanding of her.

'Where were you born?' I asked her during one of our conversations about babies.

'Know' Woo' Par' Nursery,' she answered.

'And whose tummy were you in before you were born?' This was how she talked about unborn babies.

'John's tummy.'

'No. Don't be silly.'

'John a boy?'

'Yes. Whose tummy?'

'Mi' Campbell,' she replied.

'Who's Miss Campbell?'

'Oh, Auntie Sylvia.'

Julie had no conception at all of family relationships. She believed that all babies came from Knowle Wood Park Nursery, and she would not accept that babies were looked after by their mothers. She never played at being a mother, and dolls held no interest for her.

Julie did, in fact, come from quite a large family. She had a mother and father, though she would never have recognized them as such. She also had seven brothers and sisters who were strangers to her, but who had, in a way, played a very significant part in her destiny. The Lincolns were a problem family well known to the social services. Even before they had children the Lincolns had found it difficult to cope with life and with each successive baby life became harder. Julie was the third child and, while Mrs Lincoln was having her fourth, Julie together with one of the other children, was taken into care. So, at the age of ten months she was placed in Knowle Wood Park, a residential nursery, and was kept there for a short period until her mother was able to take her back. She spent a second short term in care at the age of twenty-two months when her mother was nearing the end of another pregnancy. Back home she went again to her mother who by then had five children, all under the age of six, to look after. Quite soon her mother was pregnant again and finding it impossible to look after the children she already had. So once more a couple of the children were taken into care. When she was almost three years of age, Julie began her third term at Knowle Wood Park, but this time she was not to return home. She was one child too many.

Most of Julie's brothers and sisters are still living with their mother and father. They all attend schools for educationally subnormal children, but they are backward rather than mentally handicapped and, compared with Julie, they lead fairly normal lives. I know very little about their emotional development or their personalities, but I do know that a number have severe difficulties.

At the age of four Julie was placed in a children's home designated as a 'family group home'. She lived there for the next four years in the care of Miss Campbell and her staff. This was a home for around eight children, all of whom were 'normal' in so far as the children who come into the care of the social services can be called normal. The home was in a large, detached modern house which stood in its own garden. The number of children cared for was small enough for the staff to take on parental roles, and the children addressed each as 'auntie'. When Julie arrived at the children's home she had developed no specific behaviour problems, though she was notably retarded and had no speech apart from the word 'No'. Photographs of her taken at that time show that she was a physically normal and very pretty little girl with a ready smile.

Julie also began to attend Coventry House School. This establishment was not under the Education Authority at that time, and was not staffed by trained teachers. The children there were designated as 'uneducable'. They were suffering from the worst of mental and physical handicaps, and were very similar to the children with whom Julie was later to live at Linwood Side Hospital, in the school of which I met her. The children's disabilities meant that they were entirely dependent on other people. She was taken to the school by ambulance, and was the only child from the home who went to this type of school. It was hoped that she would develop well and soon be able to attend a school for more capable children. This was not to be.

As Julie progressed and began to learn, her problematic behaviour, or 'quirks' as Miss Campbell called them, started to develop. These quirks had begun at school and gradually she had brought each one back into the home. Her problems had grown slowly and insidiously. She had built one on top of another, rather than replacing one with another. The more that was done to contain her problems the worse they became. She had used each of her quirks to make herself dependent on certain people. She would eat, swallow, go to the toilet, and even move only if she were made to do so by the chosen people.

'Bladder swollen,' Julie said.

'When?' I asked.

'Oh, like dis,' she said holding her hand away from her stomach to show how swollen it had been.

Her control over her bladder and rectum was phenomenal. She refused to go to the toilet for so long that at one time it was thought she would have to be operated upon in order to empty her rectum. Her bladder, at times, was so full that it was clearly visible.

'Tie to toilet,' she said to me one day as I waited for her to finish in the lavatory.

'Tie what to the toilet?' I asked.

'Tie Julie to toilet.'

'Have you been tied to the toilet before?'

'It i',' she said laughing.

'What with?'

'Oh, harness.'

'A harness?'

'All day,' she nodded.

'You mean they kept doing it?'

'Tie to toilet all day.'

'You mean you were tied to the toilet all day?'

'It i',' she said screeching with laughter. 'Oh, custard,' she blurted out.

'You ate custard?'

'It i'. Eat custard on toilet.' Her laughter was uncontrollable.

She had begun to refuse to eat. It started with her demanding to be fed. Then she refused to eat food unless it had been cut up and mashed, and finally she began to refuse to swallow and spat out the food. Swallowing became the problem. Julie added to the problem of not being able to swallow food by not being able to swallow at all. She began building up saliva in her mouth and would only swallow when touched by someone. At first anyone could touch her and she would swallow, but then she would only swallow when certain people touched her; otherwise she spat out her saliva. She was told that spitting was a 'dirty' thing to do and that it spread germs about, and this made her spit even more. If spit was dirty and had germs in it, then she was not having it in her mouth. Eventually her spitting was accepted and she was given nappies to spit on.

'Julie play with herself?' she asked.

'You used to do,' I answered.

'Who Julie play with herself for?'

'I don't know. You tell me.'

'Don't like middle,' she said, her face contorted in revulsion.

'Why didn't you like your middle?'

'Middle dirty,' she answered.

The development of her masturbating habit seems to have coincided with her refusal to wear clothes and in particular to wear knickers. At one time at school Julie would strip off completely and spend much of the day naked. In an effort to keep her in clothes she was given cat-suits to wear.

Perhaps the most bizarre and frightening of her quirks must have been her refusals even to move. It had started with her choosing certain places where she would stand for hour after hour with her heels up against the wall and her head bent spitting.

She remembered it well.

'Who stand like dis for?' she asked. She had stood herself against the wall to show me the stance that she used to take up. She looked like a lifeless body hung on the wall by a peg.

'I don't know.'

'Don't like heels on floo'.'

As can be imagined, the changes in Julie's behaviour made life a nightmare for Miss Campbell and her staff at the children's home. She had changed from a manageable child into a monster and manipulator with whom they could hardly cope. When she took to soiling her bed every night and refusing to stay in her bed when Miss Campbell was off duty she had to be transferred.

'Oh, Auntie Jean,' she said once after I had shouted at her for misbehaving.

'Who's Auntie Jean?' I asked.

'Auntie Jean shout at me.'

'Oh, and what did she shout at you for?'

'Tie in bed.'

'Tie in bed?' I asked.

'Kept gettin' up.'

'She tied you in bed because you kept getting up?'

'It i'.'

'Well what did you get up for?'

'Not tigh' enough,' she replied.

'Because she didn't tie you in tight enough?'

'It i'.'

Miss Campbell asked for psychiatric help for Julie but her request was turned down on the grounds that Julie was mentally handicapped. Miss Campbell did not believe this, and maintained that she was only too clever and quick when it came to misbehaving. Despite all Julie's troublesome ways, Miss Campbell was sorry to see her go.

Julie was moved to Rose Hill Hostel, which was a hostel for approximately ten severely subnormal children, and she also began to attend the school attached to the hostel. At the age of nine she was spending all the time — at the hostel and during the day — amongst the mentally handicapped, instead of just being with this type of child at school. The hostel was a new, purpose-built place with quite a large ratio of staff to children. The social services seemed to take quite a pride in the care that was provided at Rose Hill Hostel. New efforts were being made to keep as much contact as possible between the children and their parents. The children had their own bedrooms and the policy of the hostel was to create a strong family atmosphere.

At first things were not too bad for Julie at Rose Hill, particularly in her new school, where Miss W, the head-mistress, and Penny, her teacher, were very sympathetic towards her. They invited Mr U, an educational psychologist, who was interested in behaviour modification, to help them to devise a programme for Julie. It involved rewarding her for good behaviour and ignoring her bad behaviour. The reward was a ride on a pair of roller skates which were bought specially for this purpose. As part of the programme Julie was persuaded to stop spitting for a period each day. These periods of non-spitting increased to about ten minutes a day, though she still did not swallow.

Penny did a great deal to help Julie. It was Penny who gradually weaned her away from standing against the wall by giving her the individual attention that she so craved. It was Penny, too, who worked on Julie's eating problem. She devised the method of 'pretend drink' by using an empty cup to get her to swallow each mouthful of food. Another thing Penny succeeded in doing was to entice Julie to drink her own saliva. She got her to spit into a mug and then they examined the saliva together. Julie was amazed that it was not 'dirty' and that she could not see germs swimming about in it. At a time when it was thought that Julie was incapable of relating to another person, she was forming a close attachment with Penny.

When a new matron took over the Rose Hill Hostel, Julie's situation changed. The new matron's prime concerns were hygiene, efficiency and obedience, and in all three Julie was by far the worst offender. A war of attrition gradually took the place of the family atmosphere. The saliva began fountaining out of Julie and she began to masturbate so much that holes were worn through the crutches of her cat-suits. She varied her habit of soiling her bed each night. She began to tell the staff where they would find it in the morning; on the window sill, in the wardrobe, smeared on the wall-paper. She always kept her word. When she was pinned into 'training pants' specially made for her out of the strongest material, she managed both to remove them, and to tear them to shreds. Soon she was no longer allowed in the sitting-room with the other children, where her spitting had soaked the carpet so many times that it had eventually to be destroyed. Julie became aggressive towards the hostel staff and the other children. Kicking was her method of attack. She began to spend increasingly longer periods of time confined to her bedroom. There, in her isolation, she turned her aggression towards herself. She sucked, chewed and gnawed at her finger until it became painfully swollen. In her fight against the new regime of the hostel she refused to do anything for herself and made it as difficult as she could for anyone else to do anything for her.

Julie's move to Linwood Side Hospital was wholly due to pressure from the hostel. The matron complained many times to her superiors that Julie was a child who could not be coped with in a hostel environment. Eventually, a meeting was convened and a temporary move was agreed. Probably the move was designated as temporary in order to appease the school staff. Julie had no bags to pack. She had ruined all her clothes and destroyed any toys she had. As she stood in her bedroom, with her back to the wall, on the morning she was to go, her bed was stripped and her mattress carried out to the incinerator. At the meeting it had been decided that no one from the hostel or school should visit her at the hospital, and Penny, in particular, was advised not to go. (Thankfully, later she ignored this advice.) This was to have been a total change for Julie, with nothing and no one remaining with her from her eleven years of life, apart from her memories.

Chapter 5

Julie suffered from almost the whole gamut of maladjusted behaviour problems. She lied. She swore. She was, at times, aggressive towards other children, her supervisors and herself. She destroyed property, particularly her own. She had not developed into an emotionally self-supporting child and her relationships with other people were very superficial. She lived by refusal and confrontation. She hated and feared and, in return, she was hated and feared as being an affront to human nature. Her over-dependency and endless demands for attention were the powerful force that she used to attract people, yet she repelled them with an equally strong force of rejection. In her personal relationships, as in everything, she was not just afraid of failure, she was terrified of it.

On top of these problems, which are quite common among disturbed children, Julie had developed a battery of idiosyncratic behaviour problems: her refusals to swallow, to go to the toilet and to eat; her constant masturbation; her refusals to sit down and even move. She refused and was negative to such an extent that she never used the word 'yes'. She would use repetition, or say 'It i" or 'Di" to answer in the affirmative, but she would never say 'Yes'. I asked her once just to say the word and she would not. She became very anxious about it. 'No. Like no better,' she said. The best I could get from her was a very breathy "es', and that with many tears. Her aversion to the word 'Yes' was so strong that she always said 'day before' rather than 'yesterday'.

Her intelligence was something of an unknown quantity. Her IQ was tested while she was at Rose Hill and found to be round about 60, though her behaviour prevented any exact measurement. She was certainly not severely subnormal. Severe subnormality involves having IQ below the level of 50 and, though the picture is not clear-cut, it is often the result of a pathological condition. There is usually a hereditary or constitutional factor, or the condition is the result of disease or injury. Julie suffered from no such clinical condition and it was generally accepted that she was subnormal rather than severely subnormal. The severity of her behaviour problems far outweighed the problem of her retarded intelligence. It was the social and environmental factors that were predominantly important in the development of her condition.

During Julie's first four years she did not have one unbroken year in the care of either her own mother or someone acting as a mother to her. She was shuttled back and forth between her home, where her mother was busy with her other children, and the residential nursery, where she was cared for by a number of 'caretakers', whose prime concerns were physical hygiene and health. The attention given to her during those important formative years could only have been minimal. The security, consistency and stimulation that a child needs to develop normally were not there. What possible chance did she have of developing to her full potential? What kind of basis is this lack of minimal attention for the development of trust in a child? How can a child gain any sense of security and consistency in a world of insecurity and inconsistency? It is easy to see how she developed the strategy: reject before you are rejected. Until she reached Miss Campbell there was no one to whom she could consistently relate, and by then the seed of her maladjustment was planted.

In the environment of Coventry House School, Julie's problems had flowered. Here she was labelled, not just as retarded or even subnormal, but as severely subnormal. She watched her 'classmates' being cleaned up, being toileted, and being fed. She watched some masturbate, and she watched others salivate. She saw children who could not walk and whose limbs were stiff with lack of use. Maybe it was to get attention, or maybe she was behaving as she thought she should, but whatever the reason, Julie began to copy the behaviour of the children at Coventry House. At first, efforts were made to counter Julie's refusals, but the more they tried to make her do things, the more she believed that she could not. The most common explanation of Julie's behaviour was that she was an 'attention-seeking' child. Possibly there was some truth in this explanation, though if a child needs to adopt such painful and obnoxious behaviour to get attention, then it must be a bad reflection on the care given to that child. I believe that Julie went further than 'attention-seeking'; she actually identified herself as a severely subnormal child. She said it herself many times: 'Can't. Julie handicap'.' As she stood, hour after hour, spitting, and as she tussled with people who tried to feed her, she was not simply being awkward to gain attention, she believed that she could not swallow. As she sat hour after hour on the toilet, she believed that she was physically incapable of relieving herself. Her subsequent move to Rose Hill and their failure to cope with her in the hostel there must have really set the seal on her behaviour problems.

The main causes of Julie's condition were the inconsistency of care in her early years, and her reaction to being placed with severely handicapped children Of the first of these, one can say unreservedly that it should never have been allowed. The Lincolns had been permitted to use the residential nursery as a kind of pawn-shop for their children, packing them into care when times were bad, and claiming them back when times improved. It is still the policy of the social services to make every effort to keep children with their real parents. In many cases this must be a worthwhile policy but, as had happened in the case of Julie, there is the danger of creating the long-term problem of caring for a highly disturbed child while solving the ostensibly short-term problems of the family. What a different child Julie would have been if, at the age of ten months, she had been taken permanently into care and perhaps placed with foster parents or even adopted, instead of waiting until the damage had been done. Of all the violence that can be perpetrated against a child, deprivation of a consistent mother-figure is probably the most harmful.

Julie's placement amongst severely handicapped children, at Coventry House, had had disastrous effects. It was this that had made her behaviour patterns so extremely bizarre and perverted. To have placed a disturbed child, or even a potentially disturbed child, among such children, and to have kept her there even when the damage being caused was becoming apparent, were dangerous mistakes. Yet the mistakes in both the care and education were repeated when Julie was placed first at Rose Hill and then at Linwood Side Hospital. Specialization in care and education can increase the amount of help and resources allotted to children in difficulty, but it can also label the children as 'maladjusted', 'subnormal' or 'severely subnormal', and can lead to an increase in or consolidation of behaviour problems. When a child is repeatedly misplaced the effects can be pernicious.

The story of Julie, and of the children like her, is the story of the consequences of society's mistakes in caring for children who have been deprived of a normal home. It is my belief, and the belief of many who dealt with Julie for any length of time, that she could have been a normal child; and yet, by the age of eleven she was incarcerated in a hospital for the mentally handicapped, living on a ward of severely subnormal children, and she had behaviour problems that were, in the words of one psychiatrist, 'verging on the psychotic'.

Chapter 6

Like many other hospitals for the mentally handicapped, Linwood Side lay well away from any built-up area. Its grounds were spacious and well kept. It was stone, built in the late-nineteenth century as a workhouse. Linwood Side was comparatively small, having only six wards and catering for about two hundred patients.

C Ward was the nursery ward. Walking on to this ward one was always struck by its strong, pungent smell, its clean and tidy floors, and its church-like high ceilings and windows. The largest of its two dormitories, which comprised most of the ward, was lined on either side by 'hospital beds' and lockers. This room served as a day-room, and here the children spent most of their time. The ward coped with about twenty-five handicapped children, none of whom had speech, none were toilet-trained, only a handful could feed themselves, none could dress themselves, and many were bed-ridden. As in general hospitals, the nurses wore uniforms and worked shifts. Running the ward as efficiently as possible meant adherence to a fairly strict routine of meal times, 'potting' times, bathing times, and drug administration. Between these activities there was plenty of bed-making or laundry to be sorted.

C Ward was Julie's new home.

'Smells,' she told me.

'What smells, Julie?'

'C War'.'

'Does it?'

'Oh, business on floo',' she said.

'Oh,' I said.

'I' stink,' she said. 'Who Sandra do business on floo' for?'

'I don't know.'

'Oh, she handicap'.' she said, answering her own question.

Julie's behaviour problems were contained, rather than treated on C Ward. Her continual masturbation could be ignored. Masturbation was quite common among the children anyway. The spitting was, naturally, disliked, but since the floor was lino covered and mopped twice daily with disinfectant it caused no extra hardship. There were no fitted carpets to ruin. The eating problem was partially solved by the special diet, though the nurses did have trouble getting her to swallow it, and it was supposed to be supplemented with other food. Still, there was always, what one nurse called, the 'hard way' of getting the food down. They used enemas to help loosen Julie's bowels and when this failed she had her bowels opened manually, which was something new, even for Julie. She already knew of senna pods, suppositories, laxatives, and enemas, but 'manual' was a new word to her. For months afterwards Julie would greet the sister of C Ward by asking her for a 'manual'.

A meeting was held in mid-September at which Julie's status in the hospital was changed from being temporary to being permanent. The matron of Rose Hill Hostel, who did not attend the meeting, had barred the doors of the hostel to Julie. Miss W attended the meeting to argue for her to be placed in a different hostel so that she could still attend Rose Hill School, where so much had been done for her. She even brought along an educational specialist from her area to help argue her case, but it was not to be. Dr C, the consultant psychiatrist, maintained that Julie could not be coped with in another hostel and that another failure would only cause further harm to her. So, Julie was to live in the hospital for mentally handicapped patients, and the only concession which Miss W managed to get was an assurance that there would be a full meeting to reassess the situation in December.

'Why?' Julie asked when I told her that she was not returning to the hostel.

'It's because the matron did not like you spitting,' I answered.

'Do like hostel now,' she said. 'Who sleep in Julie's be'.'

She was upset but there was not the flood of tears which I had expected. I suddenly realized that she had never really believed that she was going to return to the hostel. She had been hurt, hurt deeply, but the damage had been done six weeks before when she had left the hostel. I was soon able to change the conversation to the subject of the 'special nurse'.

One positive change that emerged from the meeting was that she was to be treated as a special case, and a nurse was to be employed specifically to look after her. The nurse was to be a parental figure and every effort was to be made to ensure consistency in the care of Julie. There was to be a real change in the hospital's approach to coping with her. The enemas and manuals were to stop in order to give her a chance of moving her bowels herself. She was to eat separately with her special nurse, and even be allowed to help prepare her own food in the kitchen. She was to know who would be meeting her when she returned to the ward from school. It seemed that all the impersonal institutional aspects of care were to be minimized and Julie was to receive the sort of care which every handicapped and special child should receive.

'You're going to have a special nurse,' I told her.

'Don't like nurses,' she sneered.

'Well you'll like this special nurse. She'll look after you every day.'

'Who need for?' she asked, showing little interest.

'You'll be able to cook your own food with this nurse and she'll take you out in the evenings. Wouldn't you like that?'

'It i',' she said and began to get interested. 'Where special nurse? What called?' she asked.

It turned out that the nurse was called Brian. There never was an extra nurse but, instead, two nurses one for each shift who already worked on the ward were asked to be 'special' to Julie. This was an extra duty on a ward which was already known for its hard work. On the Saturday morning on which the scheme was to take effect the two nurses found not only that they were on the same shift, but also that they were the only nurses on duty on C Ward that morning. They had a ward of about twenty-five handicapped children to look after: they had to change their beds, feed them, dress them, 'pot' them, give out the drugs, and on top of that they had Julie. Brian, being the junior of the two nurses, was given the extra task of seeing to Julie.

'Who special nurse?' Julie asked on the following Monday.

'Brian,' I answered.

''snot,' she said.

'What do you mean 'snot?'

'No, s'not special nurse.' She frowned. 'Don't like nurses,' she said vehemently.

'You like Brian don't you?'

'No.'

'You do, don't you?'

'It i'.'

'Did Brian feed you this morning?'

'Don't like Bwian.'

'Give over. You just said you like him.'

'Don't like hospital foo',' she whined.

Julie voiced her dislike of the hospital loud and long. She suffered from fits of depression during which her dislike would turn to hatred. At least once a day Brian would find that she had crept away to a corner where her head would be bent low in the blackest of depressions. With tears streaming down her cheeks Julie would masturbate and spit up a storm. As Brian approached to comfort her she would start to screech in blind hatred, 'Don't like hospital', 'Don't like nurses.'

Julie's feelings towards the other children were complex. She was attracted and at the same time repelled by them. She knew the name, and could even do a recognizable impression, of every child on the ward. Yet she never approached them except on the occasions when she became violent and kicked them or pulled their hair. Of all the children it was the most physically handicapped she talked about most.

'Oh, Tiny Teddy,' she said.

'What about him?' I asked.

'Oh, ribs stick out,' she reminded me.

'So what?'

'Oh, like dis,' she said showing me with her hand the shape of Tiny's rib cage. Tiny was fifteen and looked like a thin crooked baby. He was no more than three feet in height.

'Who Tiny can't walk for?' asked Julie.

'Well, because he's handicapped,' I answered.

'Why?'

'He was born that way.'

'What for?'

'I don't know, he was just born that way.'

Her attitude towards the other children made things difficult for Brian. Try as he might to encourage Julie to join in, as he played with the children, all he would get was a child writhing on the floor after being kicked by Julie.

She was her own worst enemy. Even the smallest everyday action or task was regarded as a fit battleground. Dressing could be an endless struggle with her. Brian was always kind and very patient with her, allowing her to choose her clothes and dress herself. Yet Julie could never do it. She would choose a vest and jumper from the other children's clothes, as she had none of her own, and with some persuasion would begin to put them on. When they were halfway on she would pull them off. She had a host of reasons of course; 'Too big'; 'Too small'; 'Too tight'; 'Want red one'. When Julie had to get dressed to go to school Brian would use all kinds of tricks and incentives to try to satisfy her. She would arrive at school wearing anything up to five vests, three jumpers, and two cat-suits, even though it was summer. Sometimes the straps of her cat-suit would be fastened 'cross-ways', and other days she would arrive with her arms inside the cat-suit, which was a method of dress known, between Brian and Julie, as 'The Prisoner'. She always refused to wear knickers and would scream at the mention of them.

Julie's extremely awkward behaviour, her constant rejections, and 'dirty habits' meant that she was regarded by many as repulsive and unwholesome. Her attempts at attention -seeking were seen as the behaviour of a spoilt child. Brian began to come under some criticism from his fellow nurses. They began to ask why Julie should get more attention than the other children, and also said that she only misbehaved because she was looking for attention. They considered that pandering to her demands would only make her worse. Her behaviour seemed so purposeful. Their job was to look after children who could not look after themselves, which was difficult enough without having also to pamper a child who was obviously intelligent enough to look after herself. My relationship with Julie did not help matters either; too many times she would drive a nurse right to the edge of her patience and then start squealing, 'Want John. Want John!' The fact that she swallowed when she was with me made her spitting on the ward harder to accept too. No one could understand the amount of work and attention which was needed to keep her swallowing. Finally it was decided that Julie's privileges were no longer acceptable. She was banned from using the kitchen, and when Brian was off duty she was treated just like all the other children. No attempt was made to give Brian the time he needed for helping Julie, and he was even occasionally sent to work on other wards when there was a staff shortage.

'What are you so upset about, Julie?' I asked.

'Don't like nurses,' she answered, tears gathering in her eyes.

'You are silly, Julie. You've been miserable all day. Now tell me what's wrong.'

'Don't like knickers.'

'Give up, Julie. You're wearing them, and they're not doing you any harm, so just shut up about them.'

'Who don't like knickers on bottom for?'

'What's wrong, Julie? Isn't Brian taking you out tonight?'

'It i'.'

'Is he?'

'No.'

'Isn't he on duty tonight?' I asked, realizing what was wrong.

'Who Brian not on for?' she asked, bursting into tears.

Brian did, even under such difficult circumstances, manage to reach Julie. Despite the fact that there was no improvement in her behaviour on the ward, he did become what he was asked to become: special to Julie. She was always far happier when she knew that Brian would be on the ward on her return from school. She enjoyed the walks which he took her on. She enjoyed the bed-time stories he told her. She enjoyed the personal interest he took in her.

'Who Liza can't walk for?' asked Julie.

'She's handicapped,' I answered.

'Why?'

48

'Why?' I returned.

'Born dat way.' She paused and then, to my surprise, she said, 'Julie not handicap'?'

'No, you're not,' I answered.

'Who Julie live in hospital for?' she asked.

Chapter 7

One Saturday morning at the beginning of October, I walked onto C Ward to collect Julie. I found her in the dormitory rocking from one foot to another. She was masturbating and her head was bent to the floor. There was a pool of spit at her feet. She did not look out of place amongst the other children. She glanced up at me and smiled, but her head immediately bent back to the floor. I walked to her, lifted her chin, and the spitting and masturbating stopped, as if by clockwork.

'Toilet,' she said.

'OK, come on then.'

She rushed on ahead of me into the toilet, desperately pulling at her cat-suit. She sat and pressed her abdomen.

'Who go home wi' John for?' she asked, laughing with relief.

'Because I promised you, didn't I?'

'How many night?'

'Just one. I'm bringing you back tomorrow afternoon.'

'Why? What colour toilet?'

'Come on, we can talk on the way to the cottage. Did Brian pack a bag for you last night?'

'It i'.'

'Well let's go see the nurse then.'

'Who no knickers for?' asked Julie warily, grasping my hand.

'She hasn't opened her bowels for a week,' I was told as I took the bag from the nurse.

'Manual,' Julie burbled through the gathering saliva.

'Goodbye, Julie,' said the nurse, but Julie ignored her.

Once outside I thrust her hand to her mouth, she swallowed and we ran hand in hand down the drive.

Dr C had given me permission to take Julie out; her parents did not even have to be contacted. With the backing of Dr C, I could take her home with me whenever I liked, provided the ward was notified in advance.

I lived in a cottage with Jade, my wife, and Henry, my brother-in-law. It was one of a row of cottages which stood on the brow of Sunny Hill, looking across a valley to the mill chimneys of a small town.

I opened the door and Julie burst in dragging me after her.

'Hello,' said Jade.

'Where toilet?' Julie asked me.

'This is Jade, Julie. Please say hello to Jade.'

'Where dunna sleep?' She spoke to me again.

'Look, Julie, say hello to Jade,' I said.

'Hello. What your name?' she asked as I made her swallow and turn her head towards Jade.

'Hello, Julie.' Julie was not listening; she was kneeling down lifting Jade's trousers.

'What colour shoes?'

'She likes shoes,' I told Jade.

'Don't like dese shoes.' Julie never just simply gave opinions, but spoke as though she was repulsed by the sight of the shoes.

'Oh,' said Jade, stepping back a little.

'Heels doing down,' she said trying to pick up Jade's foot.

'Pardon?' said Jade.

'Who heels doing down for?'

'She means that your heels are worn down,' I said yanking Julie on to her feet.

It was Penny who explained Julie's preoccupation with shoes to me. She pointed out that Julie had had her head bent to the floor for years, and consequently saw nothing but feet. She knew people by their shoes rather than by their faces.

That morning was the morning of the 'iceberg'. After Julie had been given the opportunity of moving her bowels herself she had soiled her bed, and then she had begun retaining it. She had not, as yet, used the toilet properly.

'Stomach hur',' she told me. I was trying to get her ready to go for a walk. After only an hour at the cottage we were already at a loss as to how to amuse her.

'Oh?' I asked.

'It stuck,' she said, and looked about nervously.

'What's stuck?' I asked as she thrust my hand fiercely to her abdomen.

'John feel it,' she moaned.

'Would you like to go somewhere?'

'It i',' she said still pressing my hand to her abdomen.

'Where, Julie?'

'Toilet,' she admitted at last.

We rushed upstairs, and she sat on the toilet pressing her abdomen and giving low moans of pain.

'Won't come,' she groaned. 'Stuck.'

'Go on, Julie,' I encouraged her.

'Can't.'

'Come on. Press, really press.'

'You do it.'

I leant over and pressed her abdomen with my thumbs. She cried out. It was true, I could feel something hard in her stomach. Her eyes bulged and her face alternated between pain and pleasure, desperation and laughter.

'Coming,' she said, getting her breath back.

'That's a good girl. One more push, and it'll be out.'

She gritted her teeth, and tears streamed down her cheeks with the effort. Then, after a bellow of pain, she laughed with relief.

'Just wait,' she said, 'just wait.' Then she leapt off the toilet.

'Look,' she said, 'look.'

'Why, it's an iceberg,' I said laughing with shared relief.

'Iceberg,' she squealed, 'iceberg.' I had never seen her face alight with such joy.

'Iceberg in cottage. You said it,' she said.

'Iceberg in cottage,' I said.

After that Julie used such esoteric phases as: 'Done iceberg today', Iceberg won't come', and 'Iceberg stuck', and there have been many occasions on which we have been thankful that she has not been understood.

Her eating at that time was tortuous. She needed a sip of water to swallow each mouthful of food, after it had been

52

arduously chewed round and round. I had to sit over her, filling the spoon for her and pushing it to her mouth whenever she became hesitant. Each meal was accompanied by all the usual moans.

'You do moan a lot,' Henry said to her as he watched the fiasco at tea-time. Julie ignored him.

'Don't like mea',' she said to me.

'You said you didn't like potato but, look, you've eaten it all,' said Henry trying again, but again he was ignored.

'Hey, I'm talking to you,' he said leaning over and giving her a playful nudge. She jerked away from him and pushed his arm away.

'Don't like Henry,' she said with that tone of revulsion. I could see that Henry felt the same towards her.

'There's no need for that,' I told her. I felt angry with her for being so rude, but also sorry because she turned people against herself so needlessly.

We were decorating the cottage at that time and, since there was nowhere else for her, Julie had to sleep on a mattress at the foot of our bed. Although I already knew about her behaviour in bed I was still surprised at the speed with which the sheets were soaked with spit. She did not sleep well that night and kept us awake by swearing at us ('Piss off' was her favourite phrase), telling us that she would not wear knickers, and occasionally screaming. At one o'clock in the morning I shouted at her to try to silence her, and after that she swore at us more quietly.

On the Sunday morning Julie was miserable and distracted. She would eat nothing and the whine never left her voice. The imminent return to the hospital dominated her, and she begged, demanded, and pleaded to come to the cottage again. When we left I had to drag her through the door.

'Oh, like Jade,' she said, though she had done nothing but reject Jade's approaches the whole weekend.

'Come on, Julie. We must go,' I said.

'Goodbye, Julie,' said Jade, but Julie did not answer.

The overwhelming difficulty with Julie during the early visits to the cottage, and for a long time afterwards, was her dependence upon me. She would scream, spit and try to follow me whenever I tried to leave the room without her.

She would even become anxious if she was not either kneeling on my lap or holding my hand. Mostly she just ignored Jade, except, that is, when she saw Jade as a threat to her monopoly of me, and then she would become abusive towards her. It was obvious that she had to become more friendly towards Jade if she was to continue visiting our cottage. The major part of the problem was Julie's swallowing and it seemed that if she could 'swallow for Jade', then she would begin to relate to her.

'Who swallow for Jade for?' asked Julie.

'Because you want to visit our cottage, don't you?'

'It i'.'

'Well it isn't just me who lives at the cottage. Jade lives there too, and you have got to behave with Jade or you won't come to the cottage.'

'Want cottage,' she said.

First there was the problem of being left alone with Jade for a few minutes. Jade had to hold her until I returned, and after a couple of times Julie began to accept this. She would stop with Jade without spitting or screaming, but yet, try as she might, Jade could not get Julie to swallow. Keeping the saliva under her tongue, Julie would open her mouth and say, 'It's gone'. Once or twice her wide-eyed innocent look fooled Jade, but the truth was she had no intention of 'swallowing for Jade'. She had me and she did not want anyone else.

A few fruitless attempts were made when the three of us were together. Julie, much to her dislike, knelt upon Jade's lap. Her frightened eyes were fixed on me. Jade tried to read to her, but it was hopeless.

'Her mouth's full, Jade,' I said.

'Do you want to swallow, Julie?' asked Jade.

'No,' Julie gurgled, looking at me. 'Can't swallow for Jade.'

Without any real belief that she would succeed, Jade took Julie's hand and pushed it to her mouth.

'Can't. Don't like cottage,' she screamed.

Jade pushed her head back shouting, 'Swallow, Julie. Swallow.' Julie's eyes filled with tears and remained fixed on me. Jade released her.

'It's hopeless, John,' she said.

'Carry on reading and try again in a minute.'

54

'Piss off,' hissed Julie coldly.

It was Jade who struck on the idea, which we really should have thought of in the first place, that Jade had to be alone with Julie away from me. A walk out together seemed the best solution.

'Do you want to go to Neil's house?' Jade asked.

'It i',' Julie answered.

'I'll take you then.'

'Want John,' she whined.

I helped her on with her coat. It was as if she were being sent to her doom rather than for a half-hour walk. I prised her clinging hands away from me, and pushed her through the door to Jade.

'Don't like Jade,' I could hear her screaming down the road as they set off for Neil's house.

Julie did manage to 'swallow for Jade,' but there was no joy in the progress. Time and again Jade had to force Julie's hand to her mouth as hard as she could before Julie would swallow. She baited Jade by holding some saliva out on the tip of her tongue to show her that she had not swallowed. This was a very annoying tactic which she had used with me in the early stages. When Jade brought her home she just handed Julie back to me.

'She did swallow,' she said, 'but I don't know whether it was worth all the effort.'

Once she had managed to 'swallow for Jade,' however, things did begin to improve. Soon she managed to 'wee-wee for Jade', 'iceberg for Jade', and 'eat for Jade', and there was a sense of achievement about these changes. She began to take a delight in being able to do things for two people and, though she still clung to me in preference to Jade, Jade was no longer just another pair of shoes.

Jade, too, began to enjoy having a child around the house. Julie began to spend more time with Jade especially in the kitchen where she watched, with interest, as Jade prepared the meals. She brought home a bag full of clothes, given to her by a friend, for Julie. It was probably the first time that Julie had had a whole wardrobe of her own clothes, and they did not have to be name tagged. There were jumpers, skirts, dresses, vests, and even fancy knickers. There were ten pairs of coloured tights too, and Julie insisted on putting all on at once.

'Fat legs,' she said, laughing at herself when they were all on, 'like fat legs.'

Jade never allowed her to wear cat-suits again in the cottage and when I brought Julie home, the first thing Jade did was to change her into her new clothes. It was surprising what a difference a change of clothes could make to a child's appearance.

Chapter 8

Some months before Julie had arrived at the hospital Jade and I had offered to foster Rose. When her screaming tantrums had become less severe I had brought her home at weekends and we had become very attached to her. We were bitterly disappointed when her parents would not give their consent and we discarded the idea of fostering a child from the hospital. However, by early November Julie had become a regular visitor to our cottage and, with the growth of her relationship with Jade, we began to talk about the possibility of fostering her. The issues seemed quite simple. Julie, like all children, needed consistency, security and love. This she could get by living with us. She would be looked after as a member of a family, rather than by people who were paid to look after her during their shifts of work. We were not particularly concerned with any long-term effects that our care would have on Julie. Her age was against any real changes. Initially, we concerned ourselves with coping with her. We knew that we could not manage her if she started spitting in the house, or if she totally refused to eat, or to go to the toilet. There was some hope, as she had already changed her behaviour in these areas in such a short time. There was also the thought that we could do little damage if we failed to cope with her. She could only return to the hospital and she would, at least, have had the experience of living in a family. We did not realize how impossible it would be for us to return her to the hospital.

I discussed the idea of our fostering Julie with Dr C. He was very sympathetic towards the idea but was a little apprehensive about whether Julie would let us look after her. He agreed to put forward the suggestion at Julie's next case conference, which was to be held on December 3, and I agreed to keep Julie at home until that time as a kind of trial period.

So she began to live full-time at the cottage. I would teach her each weekday at school and bring her home to the cottage in the evenings. This was the start of a difficult period, particularly for me, as I rarely seemed to get away from her. The only time I did leave her was during dinner break at school. At these times I had to change her skirt, which she had begun to wear to school, for a cat-suit or I would find her with her knickers round her ankles when I returned. She refused to stay with the other children and staff while I was away, but waited for me in the cloak-room where she did little else but rock and spit. Once when the class was taken out for the day I had to leave her with June for a couple of minutes. I returned to find her swearing and kicking at June, who was making ineffective efforts to hold her. The spit was flying and her knickers were round her knees, exposing her rear to all the people in the street.

At the cottage Julie was completely unable to amuse herself. She would never look at a book by herself, never play by herself, never go out, and never even go upstairs unless accompanied by myself or Jade. Her attitude was one of helplessness. Even when she dropped something, or knocked something over, she would not pick it up until she was told to do so.

Occupying Julie during the evenings was occasionally entertaining. No matter how miserable she had been at school she usually cheered up about half an hour before her bed-time. The few laughs which she gave us then helped to balance the misery of the rest of the day. It was during these times that we tried to teach her to read. We thought we would get Julie to compile her own reading vocabulary.

'Do you see these cards, Julie?' asked Jade.

'It i'.'

'I'm going to write down words on these cards, and then you can stick the cards on what they say. If I write "door" on a card you can stick it on the door with this sellotape. Do you understand?'

'Understand,' answered Julie.

'What shall we write? You think of a word.'

58

'Door,' suggested Julie.

'All right then, we'll have door first.' Jade wrote down the word, showed it to her, and Julie stuck the card on the door.

'What would you like me to write next?' asked Jade.

'Door,' answered Julie.

'We've had that word. Come on, think of another word you would like me to write.'

'It i',' said Julie becoming uninterested and scowling at me.

'How about chair,' I suggested.

'Chair,' said Julie, and the chair was duly labelled.

'Now come on, Julie,' Jade said, 'You think of one now. What would you like to label now?'

'Iceberg,' said Julie with a twinkle in her eye. 'Oh, iceberg.'

'Well give her the sellotape then,' I said to Jade, and we all laughed together.

'Iceberg' was followed by 'toilet', 'finny haddock', which was her favourite food, and 'enema', and we had to forget about the idea of labelling the objects. Yet she enjoyed the game and we found her memory to be even better than we had thought. She learnt around a dozen words a night, and remembered them almost perfectly the following night. By the end of a couple of weeks she had a reading vocabulary of fifty-six words, but by then she had lost interest and it was pointless continuing. She must have had the strangest reading vocabulary of any child.

Julie was capable of doing most of the everyday tasks, but she had to be supervised with them all, not to make sure that she did them correctly, but just so that she would do them at all. She could, for instance, dress and undress herself quite efficiently, yet she would not do so if she were left alone. I left her one night with just her nightie to put on. When I returned, five minutes later, I found her still naked, waiting for me, and poised ready to put her nightie on.

Yet, despite everything, by December 3 we felt that we were at least coping with her. She was hard work and constant work but she was swallowing, eating, and going to the toilet, and had not soiled her bed. We were, we thought, ready to foster Julie.

'Who need meeting for?' Julie asked.

'Just to talk about you, love,' I answered.

'Why?'

'I'll tell you all about it afterwards.'

'Penny coming?'

'No, I don't think so.'

'Doct' C coming?' She believed that Dr C was the man who directed her future, and she was not far wrong.

'Yes, he is.'

'John goin'?'

'Yes, I'm afraid so.'

Julie, like all children in the care of the social services, especially those who are misfits, had been the subject of many meetings and case conferences at which she was discussed; her fate was decided and, ostensibly, her problems were solved. December 3rd brought yet another case conference and yet another change in her life. There were fourteen people around the conference table: doctors, nurses, social workers, a headmistress, an education officer. There were two empty chairs, one for me and one for Julie. Also packed into that small room were at least twice as many student nurses who were there to 'observe'. As I stepped over feet to reach my seat I felt myself shrinking, and the thought that Julie was to make a personal appearance before this distinguished gathering made me feel even worse.

As questions were directed at me I explained the progress which Julie had made, and I soon came to realize that those around the table, who knew about her history, were amazed at what I was saying. She had been labelled as a child who was so disturbed that she could never change her behaviour. She would not have been placed in the hospital if anyone could have shown that there was hope for improvement. Yet, there I was, only four months after her placement in the hospital, listing the behaviour problems that had condemned her, and describing how they could be, and had been, coped with. The conference did not understand, and I did not myself fully understand, that the 'miracles' were very superficial.

Julie was sent for and led in. Luckily her performance was short and she was so preoccupied with her new yellow boots, which she was wearing for the first time, that she did not cause trouble. She even amused everyone by leaning back in her chair and resting her new boots on the conference table. No one noticed me squeeze Julie's hand under the table in an abortive attempt to get her to swallow. The two of us were dismissed from the meeting leaving them to discuss her future.

The decision that was reached was that 'the social services would look into the possibility of Mr and Mrs Swain fostering Julie'.

Julie's social worker, Mr M, saw me later that day and explained the decision to me. It meant that the fostering of Julie had been agreed in principle, and that there was only the legal procedure to follow. We had to provide the names of two referees, our doctor had to give a report on us, and the police had to be contacted to see whether we had any criminal records. The process of being approved as foster-parents can take anything up to six months, and it is only after this that fostering can take place. However, as Julie was already living with us, the process had to be speeded up and by Christmas 1974 we were approved as foster-parents.

I believe that Julie was the first child ever to be taken out of that hospital by being fostered.

Chapter 9

The idea of fostering meant nothing to Julie. We tried to explain that she was to live with us and she accepted it more or less without comment. When she did speak of it, she spoke more in terms of never going back to the hospital rather than in terms of stopping at the cottage. Six months later Julie happened to come home from school when Jade was changing her bed linen. Julie became extremely agitated and upset.

'What's wrong?' asked Jade.

'Who dunna sleep here tonight?' said Julie. She had seen her bed stripped before and she had found herself sleeping in a different place the same night. She could not believe in any permanency in her life.

Living at the cottage brought many changes in her life-style. There was no strict routine, especially at weekends, and this lack of a time-table, particularly the lack of four set meal-times, worried her. There was less structure in her life and more decisions to be made. She had to decide when she wanted to go to the toilet, when she wanted a snack, how much she wanted to eat, and even when to comb her hair and wipe her nose. The intimacy of the situation was new for her too. We slept in the same house, even in the same room, as Julie. We ate the same food at the same table as her. We used the same toilet and bath as her. There was no 'staff room' into which she was not allowed. This was not a place where people came to look after her, it was our home as well as hers.

Despite the changes in her life, no change in her attitude was brought about by simply bringing her to the cottage. She still spoke the only 'language' she knew, the language of confrontation. She fought us just as she had fought Brian, the nurses, the matron and the staff of the hostel, and Miss Campbell. The difference was that she was being dealt with by the same two people all the time at the cottage, and everything she did and said mattered. There was no opportunity for her to creep away into a corner. This gave an intensity to the situation that was stifling. Rather than being a time of getting to know each other, it was time of strength testing. There was no feeling of working together with Julie and integrating her into the family. She made it worse by being overbearingly possessive of her new things, her toys, her sweets, her mug, her plate, and even her place at the table, and also by not wanting to share anything. She expected to be looked after and be given everything she demanded, without giving anything in return.

Controlling her presented difficulties. There was a very limited choice of rewards, for one thing, and also the promise of a reward guaranteed that she would not behave. To promise to take Julie for a walk if she did not swear all morning would make her tense and unhappy and, within minutes, she would swear. Punishment, apart from physical punishment, also did nothing but make her miserable. To take her food away when she refused to eat distressed her but never improved her eating. Ignoring her had a disastrous effect. Her mouth would rapidly fill with saliva and she would say anything provoking to get our attention. Physical punishment had only a very limited effect and she soon adapted to it. A light smack worked for a while, but it soon had to become a harder smack to have any effect at all. The only control which really worked involved waiting until she lost all control of herself and then holding her and restraining her while she cried and screamed out her hatred.

Christmas time brought new problems for us, the problems of having visitors and going visiting. Just before Christmas we were visited by Jade's sister, Danny, her husband, John, and their nine-month-old son, George.

'Geor' handicap'?' Julie asked, having placed herself on my knee.

'No. Why should he be?' I asked.

'Geor' can't walk?'

'No, he can't walk, but that's because he's too small. You

63

couldn't walk when you were a baby.'

'Can walk,' she said indignantly.

'Not when you were a baby. No one could walk when they were babies.'

'Julie can't walk?'

'When you were a baby.'

'Baby handicap'?'

This was a conversation that we returned to and elaborated upon many times, as she came to redefine the word 'handicapped' and to conceive of herself as a baby.

She showed no interest in Danny or John, however, once their shoes had been investigated. She made sure that she knelt on my knee as we all sat talking and, taking no interest in the general conversation, she tried to regain my attention. She shrieked, she would not swallow and she even tried twisting my hand Before she was reduced to swearing I seized on an opportunity to divert her energies.

Danny had brought George's puzzle, which consisted of a set of rings of differing sizes and colours, which slotted together to form a cone. Julie showed some interest in it, so I showed her how the rings fitted together. With some persuasion she fitted the first three together and it was obvious that the puzzle was well within her capabilities. It was when she picked up the fourth ring correctly, that her behaviour changed. It was almost as if a black cloud had settled upon her. Her shoulders rose and she became tense and bent. She held the ring over its correct position but hesitated seemingly from fear. She then put the fourth ring down, took the third off, and attempted to put the fourth ring in the third ring's place.

'Is that right?' I asked.

'It i',' she maintained.

'But isn't that ring too small?'

'It i'.'

I have seen her repeat this type of behaviour many times since. For instance, she would do a simple jigsaw puzzle correctly for a minute or two, and again that black cloud would come. She would choose the next piece correctly, hold it over its correct position, and then appear to change her mind. She would try to force it in any way except the correct way. It seemed that she needed to fail. This was Julie the refuser.

The family's stay was too short to cause any real problems, but Julie had shown us that taking her into company was not going to be easy. We found out how true this was and just how ineffective our control over her was when we took her to stay with my parents over Christmas.

The journey there was a nightmare. She lost control of herself, spitting and screaming, much as she had done in the cave. The difference this time was, however, that it was in a crowded train of Christmas shoppers and she was not among a party of mentally handicapped children. As far as anyone else could tell, she was our child. My impulse was to ignore her and pretend that she was not with us, instead of grappling with her as I did.

We stayed with my parents for three trying days. Julie would swallow, eat and go to the toilet only under extreme pressure. We had however, expected this and were ready to deal with it. It was her attitude towards my parents that left us feeling wretched and defeated. Julie soon realized that my mother and father were good weapons to use to ensure the full attention of Jade and myself.

'Mummy,' screamed Julie. We were sitting watching television on the second evening of our visit. Julie could not last two minutes in that 'relaxed' situation.

'Come and sit on my lap,' said my mother. 'There's a good girl.'

She jumped on to my mother's lap ramming her knees into her stomach. Her glaring eyes were fixed on me the whole time.

'Careful dear,' said my mother.

'Iceberg stuck,' said Julie.

'Pardon?'

'Got diarrhoea,' whined Julie, her eyes still on me.

'Give up,' I said. I had a sickening feeling of hopelessness.

'She's all right, John,' said my mother.

She was not all right, though. Her mouth bulged with saliva and she was panic-stricken.

'Swallow,' I told her.

'Can't.' Her eyes were steely cold.

She leaned forward, almost lovingly, and whispered, 'Piss off,' in my mother's ear. I pulled her from my mother's lap and she swallowed.

'You dare say anything like that again,' I said.

Her tactics with my father were a little different. She kept ordering him to cross his legs, and would help him to do so by digging her heel in his ankle. Whenever my father refused to play the 'game' Julie would screech in indignation, 'Don't like Daddy.' Yet, if my father tried to play with her, tickling her or just talking to her, she was cold and rejecting.

Everything Julie said to my parents seemed to be directed through them at us. Probably the only time she talked properly to them was when we left them to 'baby-sit' for an hour one night after she had gone to bed. Apparently, Julie got out of her bed and raced up and down the stairs, pulling all the bed covers with her.

'If you don't get back to bed, I'll fetch a stick to you,' said my father, feigning anger after many unsuccessful attempts to persuade her to return to bed.

'What colour?' asked Julie calmly, thinking that she was in for a treat.

If she had been generally happy we could have forgiven her most of her behaviour, but she was misery itself and she never relaxed. Nothing was right for her. As she opened each of her Christmas presents she scowled and whined, saying 'Don't like it,' even before she had opened the parcel.

She did appear to like my parents' pink bathroom suite but that too she was contrary about. All day she kept demanding a 'pink ba'' with 'pink water', and yet, when the time came for her to step into it, she froze.

'Not dirty,' she said. 'Don't want to sit.'

'Come on, Julie,' said my mother. 'You've been waiting for this all day.'

'Don't want to sit on bottom,' she moaned.

'After all that nagging you've been doing. Now come on, Julie, get in,' said Jade.

'It tickles,' wailed Julie pointing to herself between her legs.

Our stay brought to light a problem that we had not considered, and it was a problem that was never fully answered. We were not accountable simply to ourselves but we had the larger family and other people to think about. Why should we expect anyone else to put up with a child like Julie? If my parents had not been so patient and understanding their Christmas could have been ruined.

Chapter 10

After Christmas Julie's behaviour began to improve, just a little, in a few respects. By January, she spat only when she was in bed, and she could be left alone for short periods without resuming her spitting. She still did not swallow on her own, but, at times, she no longer needed to be touched to make her swallow. A verbal signal would suffice, and it was only necessary to count to three before she would empty her mouth. She no longer needed to have her abdomen pressed, and sometimes did not have to be accompanied all the way, when she went to the lavatory. She would go as long as either Jade or I stood on the stairs. While eating, she no longer needed a drink, or a pretend drink, to swallow each mouthful of food. She would swallow it as the next forkful reached her mouth. She would use a knife and fork herself, once the food had been cut up for her. Eating, though, was still a time of great tension, and she had to be watched closely and given plenty of attention and instructions to keep her eating. She began to do odd jobs around the house, fetching and carrying things, drying pots, laying the table, switching on the immersion heater, and helping with the cooking. Yet she would not do anything unless she was told to and, more often than not, she had to be pressurized into action.

The longer Julie lived with us, the more we saw how capable she really was and the more intolerable her attitude became. If she was capable, why did she require forcing? On and on, day after day, came the same fights over the same things. There were arguments over which clothes she would wear, then the fight to get them on her. Then there was the toilet. If we did not send her quite forcefully enough, did not speak with quite the right amount of authority, did not stand quite close enough to the lavatory, then she would not go.

She would sit poised over the toilet and wait for more pressure to be used. Then, of course, came the eating, and so it went through the day, on from one confrontation to the next. We could not win. If we went walking it was 'Too col" and 'Too far for me'. If we stayed in it was 'Want walk', and 'Where goin' today?'. Whenever we tried to relax the pressure her behaviour deteriorated rapidly and, yet, to live with the constant battles was intolerable for the family. Life with Julie felt like a dangerous game of chess. The times of relative relaxation and happiness were few, and the times of dogged misery and mutual attrition were many.

You cannot 'make' anyone swallow, eat, or go to the toilet, unless you use artificial means. Julie desperately wanted to do these things, and it was the ebb and flow of her confidence in herself which dictated the amount of pressure we had to use with her. There was no reasoning with her. To reason with her raised doubts in her mind, and she hated the words, 'it's up to you', as they did not provide the security she needed. Our confidence too began to wane. Were we expecting too much of her too soon? Was she really as capable as we thought her to be? Was she not better off in that institutionalized world that she knew so well?

By February, our nerves were all on edge and our tempers were frayed. Julie had not been sent to school, though we had been promised in December that she would be sent. I had started my job, teaching maladjusted children at an observation and assessment centre, which meant that Jade, who was by then pregnant, was left to look after her all day. The only dramatic change in her behaviour concerned her spitting in bed.

'Get out of that bed.' I spoke coldly. All day there had been no laughter or giving from Julie, and Jade had become depressed and withdrawn.

'No. No spitting,' said Julie as she leapt from her bed.

'Come on. Where have you been doing it this time?'

'No, not on hand'chie',' she said passing her handkerchief to me. For weeks we had been trying to stop Julie spitting in her bed. It seemed such a pointless thing to do, and caused so much extra washing for Jade. She obviously hated sleeping in a bed soaked with spit, and she constantly grumbled about it.

We had insisted that she stopped, and punished her for spitting in bed by giving her no bed-time drink. Over the weeks the amount of spit in her bed had decreased until there were only a few patches of wet on her sheets. We rewarded her for this by taking her into our bed in the morning.

'If you've been spitting, I'm going to smack you tonight,' I said dragging out her sheets. She had taken to pulling out her sheets, spitting on them and tucking them under again.

'No It's dry. It's dry,' she pleaded, crouching in fear against the wall.

'It is dry, Julie. Have you been swallowing?'

'It i'.'

'Well that's marvellous,' I said kissing her. 'Get back into bed and I'll go tell Jade, and we'll see about making you some hot milk and honey. Would you like that?'

'It i',' she said with a grin.

I rushed down to tell Jade hoping that it would cheer her up. When Julie achieved something good it was easy to forgive her everything else. Jade's pleasure was short-lived, however. She returned from the bedroom and said hopelessly: 'Go and feel her nightie, John. It's soaked. There's no wonder her bed was dry.'

I felt the anger and hatred rise within me. Why should she do that to herself and why should she do it to us? I climbed the stairs in a rage.

'You little bugger,' I yelled as I pulled her from her bed. 'You have been spitting, haven't you?' I pushed her roughly round the room as I shouted at her.

'No.' She cowed beneath me.

'Haven't you?' It was I who was screaming now.

'It i',' she cried.

'Do you like to be wet with spit and to smell?' I had just had an idea.

'No. No,' she screamed, terrified.

I remembered the cold baths that she had told me of: the cold baths that she had been given for soiling her bed. I had thought it a somewhat extreme measure, but suddenly it seemed like an appropriate punishment.

'Right we'll wash if off then,' I said. I pushed her along the landing to the bathroom and ran the cold water.

'Don't like it. Will swallow in bed.' She gripped the toilet in terror 'Not dis adain,' she said, tears streaming down her cheeks.

'You're vet and smelly and you're going to be washed,' I said wrenching her away from the toilet and man-handling her into the bath.

'Had it before. Had it before,' she screamed.

'Well you're having it again,' I said.

After the ducking I led her back to her bedroom. 'You'll do without a nightie tonight', I said, though my anger was leaving me.

'Like nightie,' she said.

My stomach rose as I left her room. I felt drained and sickened at the violence of my own temper. Julie seemed to be changing my behaviour more than we were changing hers. Walking down the stairs I was shocked to hear her laughing: a strange unreal cackle that had an evil ring. Had she wanted me to lose my temper?

'We can't go on like this,' said Jade, but, short of returning her to the hospital, we did not know how to improve the situation. This was not the life with Julie that we had envisaged.

The 'therapy' worked. That night, although she kept us awake until four o'clock in the morning trying to get instructions to swallow, she did not spit in her bed. Except for a lapse two weeks later when she soaked the edge of the eiderdown on our bed, and I gave her another cold bath, she never again spat in bed. This meant that there was nothing physically wrong with Julie and that the causes of her spitting were entirely psychological. She could swallow like anyone else. It helped us believe that it would only be a matter of time before she would keep her mouth empty of her own accord during the day. It gave us hope. It was good for Julie too. She was proud that she no longer spat in her bed, and she soon changed her sleeping position. She no longer slept in a ball at the bottom of the bed but lay out with her head on the pillow. We were left wondering whether the end had justified the means.

When Mr M, the social worker, suggested that we should discuss Julie with Dr C, we jumped at the idea. Though we could not see how he could help us, the opportunity of discussing her with a specialist was very welcome. Since we had fostered Julie, Mr M had visited us every two weeks, but, although he was a sympathetic ear, he could give us little advice as to how we should cope.

We saw the doctor on February 14. His first reaction, even before we had told him our problems, was to offer to take Julie back into the hospital. I do not think that anyone had expected us to keep her. The social worker admitted this to us when he explained why she had been kept on a 'short-term' fostering basis for so long. We were not, however, desperate enough to return Julie to the hospital and we declined the offer. At our request the doctor arranged for some medicine to help her to relax. He seemed reluctant to prescribe anything and his fears were justified. The medicine did nothing but dull her senses. Her behaviour and moods were, of course, the same as before, and the medicine was soon in the dustbin. A bottle of whisky would have been more use. Where the doctor really helped, was to push the Education Authority into getting Julie to school. They had procrastinated, not wanting to pay for transport to and from school. We had accepted the delays, since the only school that was suitable nearby was the one at Linwood Side, with all its associations for Julie. The doctor, however, had no reservations and 'phoned the appropriate person. His arguments were: 'Do you realize the cost of keeping Julie in the hospital?' 'How much would be the cost of keeping her in a residential school?' 'I can take it then, that a taxi will be provided.' The dispute between the social services and the Education Authority over payment for the taxi lasted another two weeks, and then the taxi was provided, but only for two days a week. The two days a week, though, was some relief for Jade.

Chapter 11

When Julie spat all day at school, instead of swallowing, it was a great disappointment to us. She reverted to the child I had met in August. Not only did she spit but she seemed to take a perverse pleasure in ensuring that Jade knew she did. Jade took her to school in the taxi, and before she was a couple of yards from the taxi she would give Jade a malicious look and spit two or three times in quick succession.

Neil, who still taught at Linwood Side, told us that Julie tried to shut everything out while at school. She responded to no one and nothing, but just spat and waited to go home. She would return to the cottage desperate to go to the toilet, very hungry, and would plead with us not to send her to school again.

The return to Linwood Side brought much talk about 'handicap". Over and over again she had been told at home that she was not handicapped, yet she was back at the 'hospital school', as she called it. I talked with her a good deal about the children on C Ward, trying to work her through her obsession. One evening I named many of the children on the ward, and discovered the indelible impression they had left on her mind. As I named each child she mimicked him or her, and I began to understand what a grotesque parade of mutilated and distorted bodies she remembered. Her mimes conveyed each child's behaviour in detail. She particularly recalled the grossly physically and mentally handicapped children; the ones who never left their beds. She remembered so clearly the exact position of their stiff, all but inanimate bodies.

Shortly after Julie started going to school she went to stay with Penny for a weekend. Her response to a whole weekend away from us was frightening and difficult to understand.

73

Penny was the only person from her past life who kept in touch with Julie, and she had been to visit us a few times at the cottage. Julie's response to Penny on her visits had been erratic. Her initial reaction on each occasion was of excitement at seeing Penny, but this would rapidly deteriorate into shoe inspecting, screeching, and rejection of Penny. 'Don't like Penny,' was all she would say as Penny left.

Leaving Julie at Penny's that Friday night was traumatic for her and ourselves. Julie became hysterical. She would not even look at Penny but clung to me as if she would never see me again. As we left Julie made sure that we saw her start spitting. It was essential that Julie swallowed with Penny. We desperately needed to know that Julie could behave with other people as she had come to behave with us. We needed a sign that the changes were real and not just superficial.

She did manage it. She spat only a few times at Penny's, and Penny rang on Saturday morning full of excitement.

'And is her behaviour generally any better than at the hostel?' I asked Penny over the 'phone.

'Oh John, you don't know how marvellous it is. She's a hundred times better.'

'It is easy to get her to swallow for you?'

'Yes, we just touch her chin, and it goes. She even does it for the little girl next door.'

'Is she eating?'

'Yes, it's so easy with her now. Even her face is so different when she's not spitting. I hadn't realized how very pretty she is. Would you like to speak to her now?'

'Yes, I would.'

'Don't like John.' Julie's familiar whine came over the 'phone, but I had an uncomfortable feeling that I was talking to a stranger. I found it difficult to make conversation.

'Hello, Julie. Are you having a nice time?' I asked.

'Been spitting,' she told me.

'Penny says you've been swallowing.'

'Spitting in bed.'

'Well all right, Julie. Are you going out today?'

'Don't like Jade.' She spoke as if Jade was totally repugnant to her.

'Give up, Julie. We'll see you tomorrow.'

'Iceberg stuck. Can't wee-wee in cottage.'

'Listen Julie, please. We'll pick you up in the morning.'

'Don't like cottage,' she said forcefully, and was gone.

'She's all right really.' It was Penny's voice again.

'I do hope so.'

'She's just testing you. She never stops talking about you and Jade.'

'Well thanks for ringing, Penny. We'll see you tomorrow.'

Julie had been a real intrusion into our relatively peaceful lives. We did not realize the extent to which she had dominated our time until we had that free weekend. We did not regret fostering her but we did look back with some nostalgia to the time when our lives had been more carefree. As soon as we collected her, however, she gave us no time to brood.

She was as hysterical about leaving Penny as she had been about leaving us.

On the Sunday morning, I had to drag her screaming from Penny's house to the car. She completely ignored Jade and everything she said to me was loaded with animosity. To make her swallow we had to push her hand to her mouth and bend her head back in a way which we had stopped doing over two months before. The first thing she did on arrival back at the cottage was to demand to be taken to the toilet, and then refuse to perform when she was taken. 'Just been' was a phrase we had hoped not to hear again. Her attitude towards Jade was the most distressing. It was as if she was trying to cut Jade off from herself and from me. Her behaviour at Penny's however, had given us an incentive to continue trying. Jade persevered and, within a week, Julie's attitude towards her changed and her general behaviour then began to improve. Her regression was difficult to accept and understand, yet there did seem to be some cause. Through her eyes we had rejected her by sending her to stay at Penny's. Perhaps she had believed that she would never return to the cottage. Later, we were to find her regressions for which there was no apparent reason a lot more difficult to endure.

By Easter, though life with her was still hard, changes in Julie were becoming more evident. She had filled out and gained weight. Her face had colour and was, as Penny had said, pretty, except when it was crumpled into a scowl, which it was all too often. Her hands no longer felt quite so cold and clammy. She walked straighter and held her head up. Her stomach was no longer bloated and even the hump on her back seemed to be disappearing.

It was at Easter that we took a trip to the city to go shopping and to visit my parents. Julie happened to be in one of her happier moods that day and we gave her plenty of attention to stop her falling into misery. Keeping her going felt like being a juggler with too many balls in the air. The journey, however, was happy. Jade played with her at pretending that it was night time as the train went through the tunnels, and she talked merrily: 'Who need sleep for?' 'You have no sleep . . .?' 'Why night?' When we arrived in the city her mood altered and she refused to swallow when we counted. 'One . . ., two . . ., three . . .,' I bellowed, but the spit remained in her mouth. I had to squeeze her hand to get her to swallow. Still, the shops interested her, especially the shoe-shops and the tailor's dummies. She like posing like the dummies, particularly the ones in uncomfortable positions. It reminded us, and her, of her imitations of the children on Ward C.

We took Julie for her first restaurant meal, a cheap midday meal in a Chinese restaurant. She was immediately on her guard. Her conversation changed, her expression changed, and even her posture changed, becoming tense and humped. Her eyes were everywhere. She was given the chance to choose her meal but, as usual, changed her mind so many times that we had to choose for her.

'Chicken make thin legs,' she shrieked as the waiter put her plate in front of her. There was no flicker of change in his inscrutable expression. I leaned over her threateningly.

'Want toilet,' she said.

'Right,' said Jade, pleased to take her out for a minute or two. Heads were beginning to turn.

The girl that returned from the toilet was quieter, calmer, more alert, and had a swollen bottom lip. She sat down to eat like a lamb. Jade looked distraught.

'I couldn't help it,' she whispered. 'She wouldn't wee so I

gave her a good push and she caught her lip.'

'It's a good fat lip.' I could not help but laugh.

'Fa' lip,' shrieked Julie. This time it was a shriek of laughter, and soon she was giggling uncontrollably.

'It's not that funny,' I told her, seeing that Jade was still upset.

'Don't kick door,' she spluttered. 'Look.' It was the waiters who kicked open the swing door to the kitchen that so amused her.

'Don't kick door.' She found it so funny that she could not bear to watch.

Halfway through the meal her mood changed again and she would eat no more. Despite this, and the swollen lip, we felt that the meal had been a success.

Later, in the market, she came across a tailor's dummy standing next to one of the stalls.

'Dummy.' She caught her breath in excitement. 'Dummy, dummy, dummy,' she said, grabbing its hand. 'Want dummy.'

'Let go, Julie,' said Jade, forcefully but quietly, trying not to cause a commotion. The dummy began to rock and its wig fell off.

'Oooo, like dummy.'

''Ere, let go of that,' yelled the stall holder.

'Like it. Like it,' shrieked Julie and fixed it in a bear-hug.

'Let go, Julie,' I shouted. By now, people were turning their heads to see what was happening.

'Leave it alone,' shouted the stall holder sounding positively menacing. In desperation Jade yanked at her and the dummy's head fell to the floor. I picked it up and we prised her away from the dummy.

'Sorry,' I said, handing the head to the stall holder. His language had become quite colourful, so we hurried away.

It was at my parents' house that Julie surprised and pleased us. Her general behaviour was as poor as ever. She had to be fed. She also needed to be threatened and, when that failed, hurt to keep her swallowing. Yet she was noticeably more active, running up and down the stairs like a yo-yo, and she took more notice of my mother. Julie talked far more sensibly with her, and appeared to be keeping as much of our attention as she needed without being offensive to my mother. Julie consented to go for a walk with her alone, and she behaved well. In particular, she swallowed when my mother touched her chin. What seemed so unimportant to my mother meant so much to us. To be independent as we wanted her to be, she needed to swallow with everybody, and eventually to swallow on her own. This was the second small step towards this end.

Previously Julie's behaviour had been accepted by people whom we visited because it was directed mainly at ourselves, and words such as 'iceberg' were just not understood. Julie had now come to seek not just our attention, but, since she had developed a little independence, she wanted the attention of others. Her main method of obtaining attention was by confrontation. This became apparent the evening when my parents took us to see my cousin, whom we had rarely visited. Julie took a liking to her, and entered her house like a whirlwind. She immediately dragged my poor cousin off to the bathroom to inspect her toilet. When we all sat down together Julie adamantly refused to sit next to me, 'John smells,' she said, and planted herself next to my cousin who was talking to Jade. Julie did not like this lack of attention from her new-found friend.

'Iceberg stuck,' said Julie to my cousin, through a mouthful of spit, as she yanked her head round to make my cousin listen to her. She continued her conversation with Jade. Jade squeezed Julie's hand hard to get her to swallow. This was a mistake.

'Got diarrhoea.' Her voice was clear and very loud.

'Julie!' I glared at her. My cousin still continued to talk to us. My uneasiness grew. I could not tell my cousin to talk to Julie. I could see what a state she was in. I sat there unable to listen, just hoping that when Julie came to the boil she would do nothing too bad. Since her mouth was full of spit she chose a physical attack, and suddenly grasped my cousin by her bosom.

'Like cousin,' said Julie as I pulled her away.

At the end of the day we were very tired, and it seemed

questionable whether Julie's behaviour was improving or actually becoming worse.

Chapter 12

To watch any child stirring her porridge, turning each mouthful round and round her mouth, whining over it for a full half-hour is wearing on the patience. To watch a child do this for the fiftieth time, especially when you have occasionally seen her eat hungrily, can drive you to tears. Julie behaved like this in her moods of misery. She would do nothing unless forced. Each breakfast Jade would watch, giving her the odd harsh word to keep her eating, knowing that she only had to shout and rage and the porridge would be gone in a minute, but wanting her to eat of her own volition. Our nerves were being stretched and stretched to breaking point. Julie, in her misery, was a master at maintaining these situations. Almost every morning she would have to be told to get up and the flickering eyes, hunched shoulders and taut pale face meant there would be hours of strife.

Nothing pleased Julie and there were so many things that displeased her. Her nagging was incessant. She would complain about a pair of trousers being too slack. Jade would take them in and then, of course, they were too tight. She complained that her shoes were hurting, on and on, until we believed that there was some truth in it, and bought her a new pair. The next day she wanted to wear the old shoes again: 'Not too tigh' now'; 'Like ol' shoes better'.

She was prone to very swift changes of mood which greatly affected her behaviour. In good moods, for instance, she was capable of asking to go to the toilet and going on her own. On bad days, she would skip from foot to foot and grasp at herself until she was told to go to the toilet, and it was in these moods that she would sit poised over the bowl waiting for some further instruction. Often she would improve in the evening but too late for Jade to appreciate it. Jade was five months pregnant and still having to look after Julie on her own during the day for three days a week.

We did discover one reason for her sudden changes in mood. She had a 'David Hamilton phobia'. David Hamilton was a disc-jockey on a radio show which was broadcast every weekday afternoon. At the sound of his voice she would burst into floods of tears and would lose control of herself. She associated David Hamilton with returning from Rose Hill School to the hostel at four o'clock, and being shut in her bedroom. I do not know whether this was the true explanation, but her fear of his voice was deeply ingrained, and certainly must have been linked with some traumatic event.

We have made many mistakes in dealing with Julie, and one of the worst was to talk to her without taking her personality and past life into account. I, rather than Jade, was responsible for this error. I would talk to Julie 'rationally' about her problems, her behaviour, and events in her life. This was how I told her about the expected baby. Instead of playing on her interest in Jade's 'fat tummy', how the baby breathed, and so on, I told her about what I felt the consequences of having a baby in the cottage would be for her. In particular I told her that she would have to behave well when the baby arrived, a seemingly innocuous enough statement on the face of it, but the menacing overtones were obvious to Julie. What would happen if she did not do as we wanted? She had seen a baby's cot take the place of her own bed in the hostel, and so she guessed what would happen if she did not behave. By telling her what would be expected of her when the baby came I planted the doubt as to whether she would even be at the cottage to see the baby. During the whole of the week following that pep talk Julie's misery was uninterrupted, and twice she reverted to spitting. On the worst of these occasions she spat while she was out shopping in town with Jade.

It was a relief when Julie was diverted from us by full-time schooling. At last, at the end of April, after four months an agreement had been reached over payment for the taxi, and she began to attend Linwood Side School for five days a week. Needless to say, her behaviour at school had not improved. Neil kept us in touch. She still spat continuously, ate nothing, and, on occasions, kicked. On one trip out with Neil she managed to kick three little old lades. They stood next to her in a bus queue. She kicked one and while Neil apologized she kicked the other two. Another odd incident involved a very retarded patient called Christopher. He was one of the older boys who remained on B Ward all day. He would squat in a corner or sit rocking on a chair. His day was broken by 'potting' time when he was cleaned up (he was doubly incontinent), and by feeding time; and, curiously, by visits from Julie. The first time she saw him Julie liked Christopher, and then she nagged each day to be taken to B Ward to see him. She would pull him on to his feet and, almost tenderly, walk him round the ward. Her 'love' of Christopher was difficult enough to understand, but her behaviour before she was banned from B Ward was even more perplexing and worrying. Neil told us how during her last visit to the ward she suddenly pulled down Christopher's trousers and grabbed his penis. It was the only time that Neil had heard any sound at all from Christopher.

'Who hurt Ch'istopher for?' she asked me on the evening after the incident.

'I don't know. Why did you hurt Christopher?'

'It i'.'

'What do you mean "It i'."? You like Christopher, don't you?'

'Ch'istopher can't walk?'

'Why?'

'Ch'istopher handicap'?'

'Yes,' I answered, and this was the nearest she gave to a comprehensible explanation.

There was hope at school, though, in that there was a new teacher, Madeline, to whom Julie had taken a liking, and who, according to Neil, had taken an interest in her.

Full-time schooling did relieve the pressure on us, especially for Jade during the day. Julie had always been slightly better behaved during the evenings and, with her being at school during the day, we could make a more concentrated effort with her at these times. We began, once more, to try to teach her to read. This time we introduced her to the Ladybird 'Key Words' reading scheme. As before, she learned quickly.

At this time in all kinds of ways Julie began to open out, to take the initiative, and to show a mischievous side to her nature. We once caught her in our bedroom with lipstick all round her mouth and face. The warmer weather made a difference, too. She liked slugs. She collected them, prodded them, watched them slither over her hands, and even thrust her prize possessions under people's noses. She seemed to know who would respond badly to them, and these were the very people she chose. Neil had rented some land down by the river and once or twice a week we would walk down to see him. Julie was interested in 'parachutes' (as she called dandelion seeds), 'frog spit', and all the changes that go with spring. Her penetrating questions took us into many topics When relaxed and interested, she had a very inquisitive mind. She would still not play outside unsupervised, but, with plenty of persuasion she did venture out of doors occasionally. She would make short sorties and come rushing back with a slug and a mouthful of saliva. Once we managed to persuade her to go to the post box on her own. Though it was only a two-minute walk, it was a new and triumphant act of self-control.

Julie's change in outlook led to the growth of a better relationship with Henry, and this greatly improved the social atmosphere in the cottage. Both of them gradually began to think that the other was worth knowing. Henry was nineteen and lively, and, when she was in the mood, he was a good source of amusement for her. He took her for short rides on his motor scooter and she loved it, always wanting to go faster and faster She managed to 'swallow for Henry' without too much trouble, though on occasions, she did test him.

'What's on floo'?' she asked Henry when they were out walking together.

'I can't see anything,' he answered.

'I think wet,' she said slowing down. Henry did not understand.

'I think someone spit dere,' she said, but Henry still did

not understand.

'Yes,' he said, 'Come on. Hurry up.'

Then she spat to convey her message. Henry was taken aback. He gave her a cuff, and she did not spit again during that walk. 'Swallow for Henry' was another forward step. Their relationship, though, depended on Julie's mood, and whenever she sank into misery they ignored each other again.

Julie had not soiled or wet her bed in the cottage, and, once she could swallow in bed, it became a place of relaxation for her. She enjoyed being in it. We decided to take advantage of this and began to insist that she kept her mouth empty of saliva when she came to our bed on a morning. Time after time she was pushed out when the saliva built up in her mouth until eventually, she kept it empty, and she was as relaxed in our bed as in her own. With the constant problem of having to empty her mouth gone we enjoyed what amounted to almost a new relationship with her.

It was whilst in bed with Julie that we tried to remedy the damage that I had done concerning the baby.

'Can Julie touch?' she asked.

'If you want, but very gently,' answered Jade.

'Who baby in tummy for?'

'It's growing ready to be born.'

'Why?'

The discussion gave way to practical demonstrations during which Julie would become pregnant with the hot-water bottle for a baby. The baby's digestive, respiratory, and blood systems would be discussed, and then she would give birth to a hot-water bottle. She gave birth many times to 'ho' water bottle baby'.

No matter how happy and relaxed she had been in bed with us, when the time came to get up, Julie's mouth would immediately fill with saliva and we would have to start telling her when to swallow. Each morning we hoped that she would forget and just carry on as she had in bed, but she never forgot. The freedom would go and the barriers would be up.

During Whitsuntide we took Julie to stay with Jade's mother for a week in Torquay. The pattern of her general behaviour was, by then, well established; one consisting mainly of fights with the occasional burst of happiness and sheer joyfulness that made us persevere. One particular problem, that was to grow to terrible proportions later, marred the visit to Torquay, Julie's continual antagonism towards Jade. Whenever she became very dispirited she would begin to ignore Jade, Julie's only comments being calculated to annoy her. This would continue until Jade forced Julie to recognize her authority, even her very existence. With the growing baby taking more of Jade's energy, the effort needed continually to re-establish her relationship with Julie exhausted her.

One of the events which compensated us was a visit to the fun-fair.

'Inflatable! Inflatable!' she squealed in ecstasy. The object of her excitement was a large polythene dome which had a huge air mattress for its base. It was called a 'Moonwalk'. Through its windows smiling parents watched their children bouncing, walking, and falling over the air mattress. Julie strained to join them. The attendant rang a bell and out tumbled one lot of children and in clambered the next lot, with Julie among them. For nearly five minutes she was indistinguishable from the other twenty or so holiday-making, tumbling, turning children. The child, who had been indistinguishable among children suffering from the grossest of physical and mental handicaps, was now indistinguishable from normal, healthy, happy children, indistinguishable, that is, until the bell rang marking the end of that particular 'moonwalking' session, and out they all tumbled, all but one. Julie sat in the far corner in defiance, a 'moonwalker' reluctant to leave.

'Excuse me,' I said to the attendant, and pulled the flap aside. I poked my head into the 'Moonwalk'.

'Come on, Julie,' I shouted.

'No.'

'Come on now.'

'No.' She was not whining. Her voice was firm, calm, and very matter-of-fact.

'Like it,' she said.

I pulled myself out, and turned to the attendant.

'She wants another go,' I said paying her the fee.

'It'll be her last,' she said miserably and pocketed the money.

I have always found that the more normal a child looks, the less acceptable is unconventional behaviour to strangers. One who looks handicapped is always regarded with more sympathy. I have always wished that I had a handout, giving a brief explanation of Julie's background, to pass around in difficult situations, so that others could appreciate the significance of her behaviour.

Again she gambolled with the other children while Jade and I watched in happy wonder. When the bell rang, she just lay down in delighted contempt of my authority.

'Could I go in to get her out?' I asked the attendant.

'No one over eighteen allowed in,' was her terse answer.

'Could she have another go?' I asked.

'There are other children, you know.' With some difficulty I kept my thoughts to myself, and opened the flap.

'Come on now, Julie.'

She gave no answer as her mouth was absolutely full of saliva, but she did not move either.

'There will be trouble if you don't get out here now.' Julie did not move. The attendant impatiently held back the other children.

'Right, I'm going then,' I said in desperation, and shut the flap. Finally, to our profound relief, she came bounding out.

Chapter 13

Madeline had expressed a wish to take Julie home for a day, and so, during the Whitsuntide holidays, we took her to Madeline's house and left her there. Her behaviour was fairly predictable. She clung to us when we took her, and rejected us when we went to collect her. She managed to keep swallowing and to eat with Madeline, but she was very demanding. The consequences of that visit, however, were far-reaching and unpredictable.

On the evening of Julie's first day back at school after the holidays, Madeline came to see us. She had been tremendously moved by Julie's behaviour at school that day. Madeline believed very strongly in the mystical side of life, and spoke of the events of that day as if they were an apocalypse to her. She had arrived at school to find Julie very disturbed, more disturbed than she had ever seen her before. Her face was contorted by her violent spitting. She had pulled down her trousers, tights and knickers, and was masturbating. She was screeching and tears were rolling down her cheeks as if something dreadful had been done to her. Madeline was at a loss. She had hoped to come into school and to start Julie swallowing, just as she had done during her visit, but on seeing her Madeline dropped all thoughts of this. The more she tried to console Julie, the worse she became. She swore, kicked, and refused to move from her corner of desolation. By mid-afternoon, Madeline had become almost as depressed as Julie, but she dragged her out of school for some fresh air in a last desperate attempt to pacify her. While they were out walking, a hail-storm broke and the sky opened in a tremendous downpour. Julie was still spitting furiously and in the heat of the moment Madeline turned on her: 'Spit! Spit! Spit!' she cried. Julie again burst into a flood of tears. 'Spit! Spit! Spit!' Madeline cried again almost in tears herself, when suddenly Julie looked up at her and said 'It's gone.' She opened her mouth to show Madeline that she had swallowed. They hugged each other in joy, and ran splashing through the puddles with Julie looking up occasionally at Madeline who would tell her to swallow.

To swallow at school meant a whole change of identity for Julie. From then on she has never reverted to spitting. During bad times Julie did not swallow and she allowed the saliva to build up in her mouth until it came spluttering out, but she never actually spat it out. None of us had realized how desperate she was to swallow. The Jekyll and Hyde existence that she had been leading, of spitting at school and swallowing at home, had been as abhorrent to her as it had been to us. Her behaviour that day had been a frantic plea to Madeline to help her to stop spitting. Her looks of hatred and her intentional spitting in front of Jade as she left the taxi each morning, were not just her retaliation for being left at school: they too, were cries for help.

A few days later we received a letter from the headmistress of Linwood Side School. This was the only formal report that we ever received from the headmistress. It dealt with an incident during Madeline's dinner-break, when she left Julie for half an hour. The letter explained: 'Julie became upset and attacked another child, biting and scratching quite viciously and she had to be forcibly restrained.' The headmistress' explanation of Julie's behaviour was that it was 'probably prompted by the feeling that Madeline had rejected her'. This might be a partial explanation, but Madeline had left Julie at dinner-times before without incident. Madeline visited us again that evening, and she had what I believed to be a better explanation. Julie had been left in the charge of a non-teaching assistant who had not seen any real need to keep her swallowing. Her mouth had filled with saliva. She did not want to spit, but was not being given the instructions she needed to swallow. In that impossible situation she lost all her self-control. The next day the non-teaching assistant was well primed to keep her swallowing. She managed to swallow when she was told to, and the difference in her outlook was a pleasant surprise for the assistant.

New vistas opened for Julie. She had enough confidence in herself not to need the spitting. I believe that there was a change in her image of herself, from 'the girl who spits' to the girl who does not spit'. At school she could be left with any of the staff, and she would swallow when instructed to do so. Quite soon after that, she began to eat at school, provided she was fed. She no longer just waited to go home, and was beginning to enjoy being at school

This development brought improvements at home. Here too she swallowed for other people. She swallowed for the next door neighbour, for Brian (who by then was living close by), for Neil, for Neil's wife, and even for Neil's eight-year-old daughter. She wanted to experiment with her new ability by swallowing with as many different people as she could. She also needed less prompting from Jade or myself before she swallowed. Occasionally she needed almost no prompting, and would swallow when she just looked at us. Her mouth would only fill to any extent when she was on her own for a while. She required less supervision in many areas. She would go up two flights of stairs and go to the toilet by herself. She dressed and undressed herself, fastened her own shoes, washed herself, cleaned her teeth, and bathed herself. She prepared drinks and snacks for herself, fetched and carried, and set the table. She would often refuse help that was offered.

Despite her improvement, she was still not an easy child to look after, and her mood could plummet into the depths of misery at the slightest stress. Yet, there seemed increasingly to be more ups than downs, and our efforts were beginning to be compensated. Certainly she had come a long way from that 'severely subnormal' child whom we had originally fostered eight months before.

There was a move to get Julie placed in a more suitable school. It was Mr M who organized another meeting, which took place on June 18, to discuss this proposal. Nearly everyone at the meeting agreed that she would profit from a change of school. Dr C suggested that she should attend our local primary school on an experimental basis. However, the people who had the power to move Julie, the education officials, were not so enthusiastic. They could see nothing in her progress which suggested a change of schooling. The only concession they made was to agree to an examination by an educational psychologist. We were never to learn what that educational psychologist's recommendations were.

Julie's appearance at the meeting cannot have helped. She was in no mood to perform that day.

'Would you like to go to a new school?' she was asked.

'Want to go to B Ward,' she answered. This was the ward where Christopher was kept.

'Do you like living with Mr and Mrs Swain?'

'Don't like cottage.'

'Do you have your own bedroom?' someone asked.

'No,' she replied, though she had been sleeping in a room of her own for a number of months.

'Do you have lots of toys?'

'No.'

She had a pile of toys which I confiscated for a number of days as a punishment. Julie often lied in this way, and it always seemed very unnecessary and thoughtless. It always hit us very hard.

During the happier period of improving behaviour Julie again went to camp for a week with the school. Her clinging as she left was as desperate as ever. 'But do love Jadie,' she said as if she was being sent away because she did not like us. Her response when she returned was also as severe as ever. She absolutely refused to get into the taxi when Jade collected her, but clung to the school railings screaming out her hatred for Jade, myself, and the cottage. This dissipated more quickly, however, and she was calm by the time she reached the cottage.

The climax of that happier period came with a couple of trips out. One was to Belle Vue Zoo in Manchester, and the other was to Blackpool where my sister and her husband lived. Her calmness and the lack of tension enabled her to be open and outward. She enjoyed the zoo. She showed little interest in any of the small, furry animals, but preferred to stare, totally engrossed, at the ugliest and largest of the baboons and apes. Her favourite baboon had a face and bottom that were matching, both having pink and blue patches. It did little else but sit motionless. She would have watched it all day if we had allowed her. While walking round Bell Vue Zoo Julie was suddenly accosted by a professional photographer, who loaded her with three miniature monkeys dressed in caps, jumpers, and trousers. When I first met Julie she was terrified of all animals. A puppy could terrorize her, and she absolutely hated any animal to touch her. This fear had diminished slowly, but had by no means completely gone and so I felt nothing but dread at seeing her with those three squirming miniature monkeys. Julie, however, took it in her stride, and even smiled for the photograph. She did try to put one of the monkeys down to see how it walked, which the photographer did not like at all but, in the circumstances, I felt it was quite a reasonable thing to do.

The day in Blackpool was a day of few conflicts and much happiness. It was there that she found her dolphin. Ever since going to camp she had wanted a large blue inflatable dolphin. She had seen a boy carrying one and for some reason it had stayed indelibly in her mind. When she saw one almost the same size as herself, in a shop along the Golden Mile, she danced and leaped in excitement. She hugged and clung to it as if it was her long-lost brother, and it became her constant companion for a few weeks. We took her, and the dolphin, to Blackpool's pleasure beach. Like any other happy child she wanted to try all the rides. The 'Big Dipper' frightened and exhilarated her so much that she was speechless, a very rare condition for Julie. It was quite a few minutes before she demanded: 'Big Dipper adain.' At last her pleasure was beginning to be unmarred and less restricted by her behaviour problems.

At my sister's, too, she needed no nasty, indirect comments or provocative behaviour to hold people's attention. She was free to explore their house of her own accord. She was so easy and relaxed that she had an accident. She tripped, fell, and broke a cup which she was carrying. It was a marked change from the strained and well-controlled movements, which we had been so used to seeing. She giggled over her tea and ate plenty, rather than as little as possible. Typically, she finished the visit by refusing to drink her cup of tea, and then demanding another, but she did not lose her high spirits.

During the next two weeks she regressed. Julie's behaviour had deteriorated many times. Some regressions were minor and involved only one aspect of her behaviour, but others were major and, within a week, months of progress were lost. Often there appeared to be no reason. It was as if she had overreached herself and she had to scurry back within her defensive wall of refusals. Possibly the regression in July was due to the decision that she was not to go to a new school, coupled with the news that Madeline was leaving Linwood Side.

The first achievement to slide was her swallowing. She no longer looked towards us to swallow, but would only do so when we caught her eye. She began purposely to look away from us, building up mouthfuls of saliva. There was no thought of spitting, but she wanted to be made to swallow. If she was ignored she would soon swear, or point to her crutch, or moan to make us look. This led to us going through all types of tricks and contortions to try to catch her eye. It meant that we had again constantly to worry about when and how she would empty her mouth. We found that we no longer had the patience or the will to think out any new ways to persuade her to get rid of the saliva, and it was so terribly easy to revert to a physical method. First she would not swallow when we caught her eye but waited until we took a step towards her; then she waited until a hand was raised in anger; and finally she waited until the hand was brought down. A slap would make her swallow, and after days of misery and furtive glancing to see whether her cheeks were bulging with saliva, the tapping and pushing started to increase. It snowballed, and when Julie was in a bad mood, and there was nothing but mutual hate between us, nothing short of a smack would get rid of each mouthful of saliva.

Next her ability to go to the toilet regressed. She would climb the stairs and sit poised over the bowl until she heard someone approaching on the stairs. Then the eating deteriorated. The hunched shoulders returned, so too the fear, and the atmosphere became as tight as a clenched fist. How bitter it was to see her cut off again; to see her close her life like a book that had only just begun to be read. All efforts to reason with her or play with her and love her produced only more misery and more tension. The physical methods we were using grieved us, but, at the time, there seemed no alternative. The thought that we were going to have to go over ground already fought and won was bitter.

With other people too this regression was all too apparent. She no longer swallowed when told to do so at school, but needed a physical cue to make her swallow. The staff began to press her nose each time her mouth filled up.

The school closed for a two-week holiday in July, and by this time Julie's mind was closed too. Jade, who was nearing the end of her pregnancy, was going to have to deal with her at home all day. The weekend before the holiday was the worst we had known. On the Saturday night she ripped a hole in her 'beloved' dolphin. She admitted that she had done it quite purposely with her teeth, and showed no regret or remorse but could only demand we buy her another. Sunday was a day of total misery. She was stooped, her face was colourless, and her eyes wild, but worse than all these was the constant talk about the hospital, as if she were remembering a happy period of her life. The day had worn us all, and as we sat in wretched silence around the tea table I felt so drained, so sickened, I could not even give her the glances she needed to swallow. Her cheeks began to bulge with food, tears appeared in her eyes, and she made what little noise she could to gain our attention. We both looked up, not in anger, but in silent resignation. Julie did not swallow; it had gone too far for that. I looked at Jade and she shrugged.

'We'll put her to bed,' I said.

'What about your parents coming?' asked Jade. My parents were due to arrive. 'What about these next two weeks?'

'It's because of what holidays meant for her in the hostel. No Penny,' I said.

'Even if that's the reason for all this, it doesn't help.'

I took a course of action that I was later to regret. I decided to give Julie an alternative, in the hope that she would make a positive choice and pull herself out of the state she was in. I wanted her to choose us and her life at the cottage and to stop talking about Linwood Side. I brought the waste-paper basket to the table.

'If you want to stay here with us, just swallow that food.

If you don't, if you want to go back to that hospital, just spit it out.' I spoke coldly and quietly. Even as I said it I knew the impossible position in which I put her. Tears streamed down, and her mouth chewed round and round in desperation. I repeated myself; a little louder this time and emphasizing the word 'swallow'. She shook her head. Her nose was running and she kept licking the mucus into her mouth.

'Go on, and spit it out. You can't swallow it, can you? Spit it out. You like the hospital and nurses, don't you? Go on, spit it out,' I shouted, trying to goad her into swallowing.

There was no response, just those frantic pleading eyes. She could hold it no longer. A little food and saliva dribbled from her mouth, then out it all came as she coughed and spluttered it into the basket.

'You want the hospital?' I said.

'Do,' she nodded.

'You like nurses?'

'Like nurses. Like hospital foo'.'

'Don't you want to live in the cottage with Jade and Henry and me?'

'No. Don't like John and Jade.' Her face was deathly, but she answered quietly and calmly.

'Well, perhaps she does want that. She doesn't want the pressure. We'll put her to bed, and call the social worker tomorrow,' I said.

Jade looked white and ill. 'I've had enough. Get her out of the cottage for a while, John. Take her to Brian's.' Brian was away and he had left the key to his house with us.

'Right Julie,' I said. 'Go and put your cat-suit on. You're going back.

Quiet and passive she changed herself. 'Like cat-suit,' she said. 'Like hospital bed.' By the time we set off for Brian's house Julie looked the part of a subnormal, hospitalized child. When we arrived at Brian's cottage I took her upstairs and sat on the bed looking at her. The threat of the hospital had been a bad mistake. She had not enough confidence in herself or in us to face that threat. She knew that her behaviour had led to rejection and, as yet, she could not conceive that her behaviour could lead to acceptance. I tried o undo the harm I had done

'Why don't you play with yourself?' I shouted. 'You're going back to the hospital. You played with yourself at the hospital, didn't you?'

'I don't play with myself now.' She said it emphatically, and used the personal pronoun which she so rarely used. I dragged her to me by her cat-suit and thrust her hand between her legs.

'Go on play with yourself. That's want you want. You want to go back to the hospital.'

'No,' she cried. The tears began again.

'Oh yes you do. You said so. You like hospital don't you?'

'No.' She was screeching by now.

'You do want to be handicapped, don't you?'

'No, no.'

'Yes you do. You'd better spit. You'll be spitting at the hospital.'

Her eyes bulged in terror.

'No I don't spit now.'

'Go on spit,' I yelled. 'I'll give you three. One, two, three.'

'No. I don't spit.'

'You don't like the cottage. You don't like John and Jade, do you?'

'I do. I like cottage now. Want to stay at cottage. It's your home.'

Tears were rolling down her cheeks, and I could feel tears in my eyes too.

'Listen to me, Julie.' I raised her face to mine. 'Say don't like cottage.'

'I do, I do.'

'Say it,' I yelled.

'Don't like cottage.' As she said it I slapped her.

'Say don't like John and Jade.'

'Do. I do.'

'Say it.'

'Don't like John and Jade.' Again I slapped her.

'Say want to go to hospital.'

She said it and I pushed her back on to the bed and held her there.

'You are not going back to the hospital. You're going to

95

stop with us, and you're going to like it, and you're going to behave. We are going to help you whether you like it or not. Do you hear?'

'I do,' she answered.

'You live in the cottage. It's your home.'

'It's your home,' she repeated.

'Well, let's go home then,' I said.

The rest of the evening passed fairly peacefully. There seemed to be a chance we could succeed in helping her, and we regained our determination to keep Julie and bring her through this difficult period.

The next two weeks were dreadful. Julie seemed to be as cold-bloodedly awkward with Jade as possible. She took every chance she could to be as offensive and as difficult to manage as only she knew how. Twice I came home from work to find Jade in tears. Julie was determined to keep herself closed, and we were only just surviving.

Chapter 14

'Where's Jadie?' asked Julie as she pushed the food I had cooked for her round and round her plate.

'Where is she, Julie?' I asked.

'Hospital.' Her shoulders were hunched and tears gathered in her eyes.

'And why is she in hospital?'

'Oh baby born,' she answered. 'Baby in Jade's tummy?'

'No.'

'Who baby not in tummy for?'

'Because the baby's been born now. Julie, will you hurry up with your tea. We've got to go to the hospital soon.'

'Want Jadie. Like Jadie now.' The flood of tears brimmed over and rolled down her cheeks.

'She won't be away too long. If you carry on playing with that tea I'm going to take it away from you. I've finished mine, and Henry will be here soon to take us to the hospital.'

'Want Jade's tea,' she burbled through her over-full mouth. 'Like Jadie now,' she said. Her face was covered with blotches and her eyes were red-rimmed. The only way I could get her to eat was to sit in front of her pushing the spoon to her mouth to make her swallow, as we had done months before.

It was the Monday after Julie's two-week holiday from school. That morning at seven o'clock Jade had been rushed into hospital. I went with her leaving Brian to take Julie to school. At half past ten that morning Jade gave birth to a slightly premature, healthy baby girl. She was to stay in hospital for the next ten days. At school that day Julie spat, or rather refused to swallow and allowed the saliva to build up in her mouth until it would come spewing out. By the time she came home she was in a very anxious state. Jade had

97

gone and her security was threatened.

That evening Madeline arrived to stay and help look after Julie while Jade was in hospital. With her arrival the pressure was taken off myself and even off Julie. She had someone new to fight against, new battles to get her teeth into. Life for Julie became quite pleasant in the absence of Jade. She came back from school to Madeline who gave her undivided attention until I came home. Then there were the regular visits to the hospital every evening when she would walk around the hospital grounds with Madeline while I visited Jade. On the Thursday she even had a day off school when Madeline took her to Belle Vue. As far as I could tell, though I saw little of her, Julie was doing quite well, though Madeline was beginning to look tired.

During her visits to the hospital Jade would come to her window.

'Where baby now?' Julie called to her.

Jade pointed upstairs to a room where the baby lay in an incubator.

'What 'bout pipe?' asked Julie. By 'pipe' she meant the umbilical cord. She scarcely waited for an answer but launched into her next question: 'Who baby born for?' 'What in Jade's tummy?'

Due to hospital rules Julie was allowed to visit Jade only at the weekend. The first time she behaved so badly that I had to remove her. She refused to swallow, ignored Jade and the baby (who was by then out of the incubator), screeched, and had to be dragged away. The second visit, though, was better; Julie was happier and inquisitive. She studied the baby, especially her 'pipe', felt Jade's tummy, listened to the radio through the head-phones, and had to be restrained from climbing into Jade's bed.

By the time the ten days were over Julie seemed to have gained some acceptance of the situation, and was generally quite relaxed and cheerful. We were not prepared for her reaction to Jade's return, and her reaction to the baby, Anna, being brought into the cottage. She knew that Jade and Anna were due home, and that Madeline would not be there that evening.

When I collected Julie from school in the taxi, I

understood her quietness to be excitement. I was too euphoric to see the danger signals. Even when she gripped the seat in front of her and had to be pulled from the taxi, I saw nothing to worry about. Jade and Anna were home — how could there be anything to worry about?

It was only when I helped her off with her coat that I saw how chronically ill Julie looked. Her face was drawn and death-like. Her back was humped and she looked shrivelled and shrunken. Jade came from the living room and greeted her.

'Don't like Jade.' Julie addressed herself to me. Her voice was flat and unemotional.

'Come on in, and tell me what you've been doing at school.' As Jade spoke she moved forwards to embrace her, but Julie stood frozen.

'Don't want to,' said Julie and again she spoke to me; again her voice contained none of the usual vehemence. She stared blankly at the floor.

'Where's Madeline?' she asked me.

'Gone home, just as I told you she would.'

'Want Madeline. Don't like Jade now.'

We ignored this comment and ushered her into the living room.

'Don't like Anna,' she said without looking at the baby who was asleep in the carry-cot.

Her lips chewed round and round working the mucus from her running nose into her mouth, which was already full of saliva. She glanced at me, but did not swallow.

'Get rid of it, Julie,' I said.

'Can't,' she told me. 'Spit got germs.' It had been so long since I had heard that phrase that I was taken aback.

'Don't be so silly,' I said. 'Get rid of it now.'

As I stepped towards her she moved away from me.

'Can't swallow,' she announced with calm assurance.

'What do you mean you can't swallow?' My voice rose a little. 'You've been swallowing for months and months.' The sleeping baby woke and started to cry.

'Can't,' she said, backing away and raising her hands as if to protect herself.

'You're going to,' I shouted. I knew she had to swallow for

her sake. I brushed her arms aside and lifted her head. When I saw her dead, glazed eyes, I felt alienated from her. Suddenly she was a stranger to me. I did not know what to say; did not know what to do; did not know how to touch her. She stared, mesmerized by a distant, terrible horizon.

'Can't,' she said. I tilted her head back with a jerk.

'Spit got germs,' she said. I put my hand to her mouth and pushed hard: she swallowed, but there was no relief in her face. It was an empty victory.

I looked towards Jade. She was comforting the baby in her arms, and she looked weary and upset.

'She looks like the child you brought home from the hospital all those months ago,' she said.

'Hospital,' said Julie.

'What about it?' I asked her.

'Want hospital,' she answered.

'Well, you're stopping here,' I said.

'Don't like cottage.'

'Give up, Julie,' I shouted at her, and she lapsed into her bitter silence.

That evening we took a walk to Brian's house. There I could not bear to see her crouching and rocking from one foot to the other just as I'd seen her do on C Ward; so I sat her down, and she sat cringing like a sick animal, staring at the floor, ignoring everyone and everything except myself and her mouth. Every five minutes I had to force back her head to make her swallow.

'She says she wants to return to the hospital,' I told Brian.

'She can't mean that, John. She could never ever want to go there again,' he said, and it was reassuring to hear. Yet all the joy of bringing home our baby and taking her to our friends was marred by Julie's pervading cloud of misery, coldness, and hostility.

Dispirited, we took her home, forced a little supper down her, and we put her to bed early that night. She had resigned from her new way of life, resigned from the family, and had erected all the old barriers to protect herself. All those improvements we had worked so hard to establish were gone. Worse than this, though, the original spark of life had gone, and she no longer looked towards us for help.

100

Our thoughts about Julie were confused and torn. We did not want to hand her back to the social services. We did not want her to think that the baby had taken her place. That could only reinforce her belief that the world was insecure, and that she could trust no one. We knew that her reaction had been caused by that fear of rejection and that she was, in her own perverted way, asking for reassurance. Yet we simply did not know whether we could give her that reassurance: she was so cold and unreceptive, and she had undermined our original fight and determination to cope with her and keep her. There was Anna too; she cried out with healthy lungs for her fair share of our attention. Like all parents we wanted everything to be right for our first baby, and the fraught atmosphere was anything but right. Our decision was that we would look after Julie, however she behaved, for six weeks, but if by that time she had made no improvement we would return her to the social services. Mr M came to visit us the next evening, and we explained to him our position. Again he told us that the only alternative, if we could not cope with her, was the hospital.

During the next two weeks there was no smiling and no laughter from Julie. We just coped with her, going from one struggle to another and there was always that stultifying mouthful. Yet there seemed to be little jealousy of the baby. Julie more or less denied her existence. The only time she took any notice of Anna was when she was being fed or changed and then she would stare with a kind of morbid fascination. With Jade she was cold and unresponsive to the point of being insulting.

'Hello Julie. What do you want?' Jade asked. Julie had appeared at the door in her nightie.

'Kiss John good nigh',' she said. 'Kiss John's forehea'.'

'If you wish,' I answered.

'Just minute, just minute,' she said as she brushed back my hair. Then she kissed me and actually smiled.

'Blimey,' I said, 'be careful Julie, your face will crack.'

'Kiss Henry's forehea',' she said, and she ceremoniously kissed Henry's forehead.

'Kiss firepla' good nigh',' she said. She crept towards it but then stopped.

101

'No, no,' she said shaking her head. 'Don't like that.' It was a pleasure to see her behaving so spontaneously again.

Then she walked around Jade to the door, hardly even glancing at her.

'Good nigh' Henry. Good nigh' John. Good nigh' firepla',' she said through the gathering saliva and left.

The only way Jade could get a positive reponse was to deal with her in the style of a martinet. The more loving Jade was the more Julie demonstrated her rejection of Jade.

A week after Jade's return Mick, a friend, came to visit us.

'Let's take a walk,' I suggested soon after he had arrived. I wanted to get away from the cottage, away from the tension that had been drawn even tighter by Mick's arrival. Julie was losing control, and she knew it. There was fear in her eyes, and her voice was reaching screaming pitch as her comments became more provocative.

'Want toilet,' she said.

'But you've just been,' I told her.

'No. Didn't do it.'

'Well come on then, and then we'll go out.'

'Just been,' she said in that familiar voice of hers.

'Come on, Julie,' said Mick. 'Let's go out. That'll cheer you up.' He grabbed Julie and tried to tickle her. She screamed and lashed out with her arms and legs.

'Piss off,' she said, her eyes on me all the time.

'Go and get your coat on,' I told her sharply

When the baby was ready we followed her into the hall. We found her standing there rigid with fear, no coat on, and a mouth full of saliva ready to bust from her lips.

'Now look,' I shouted, moving towards her. She winced, swallowed, and shrank away. Her hands were raised to protect herself.

'Get your coat on,' I said.

'Shoes too tigh',' she whined.

'Come on or we'll go without you,' I threatened.

'Too far for me.'

I opened the door for Jade to wheel the pram out, but still Julie made no move to put her coat on.

'I've had enough,' I told her. 'I'm not going to be your friend if you're going to carry on like this.'

'Oh, do want to be friend now,' she said. She moved forward and opened her arms to embrace me.

'Not if you're going to carry on,' I said, fending her away.

'Oh plea'. Will be nice. Will be nice,' she pleaded, trying to get her arms around me.

'All right then, let's be friends,' I said, and we embraced.

'Let's be friends,' she repeated, but as I released her she backed nervously away from me. 'Want toilet,' she whined. I handed her coat to her and pushed her through the door.

As we left the cottage Mick looked puzzled. He asked: 'Don't you get fed up with it all?'

'We do,' answered Jade, 'but at least she's getting some of her old fight back. She was just dead last week.'

The walk did nothing to improve things. Julie kept a yard between myself and herself. She would come no nearer, but also would go no further away. Gone were the days of slug searching and bilberry picking.

The visit of Penny was different. I had taken two weeks off work when the baby came home, and at the end of those two weeks Penny came to help Jade look after Julie for a while. Her initial reaction was to welcome Penny with open arms and to reject both myself and Jade. This soon changed, though, because Penny was not just a visitor; she had come to help cope with Julie and she realized this at the first breakfast time. It was Jade who knew the routine; Jade who knew the key phrases and the right amount of pressure needed to keep Julie eating; and it was Jade to whom Julie turned in preference to Penny. The visit worked like a safety valve, with Penny taking the buffeting.

After Penny's visit the day-to-day living eased a little. Julie had regained the confidence to go to the toilet by herself and, though she was reluctant, she would hold her own knife and fork again while she was eating. The swallowing improved too. Once again she began to look to Jade or myself for the slightest signal to make her swallow. Best of all, she did, at least occasionally, speak to Jade.

It was a time of yo-yoing moods. In the best moods she still gave precious little; in the worst she leeched her life from us. Either the moods determined the swallowing, or the swallowing determined the moods; whichever way, it was

103

always more difficult to get her to swallow when she was depressed. From the moment she awoke, on the day that we went to Sheffield to see Danny and John's new home, her eyes forecast a black day.

They came to pick us up in their car and there was so little room for us all, that Julie had to sit between my legs. She immediately started wriggling and squirming against me.

'Sit still please, Julie,' I said.

'It tickles,' she said, pointing between her legs.

'Don't start,' I pleaded.

'Not uncomfortable,' she screeched and rammed herself against me (Julie always mixed up the words comfortable and uncomfortable.)

'That hurts,' I told her.

'Want to kneel up,' she screamed.

'Stop it, Julie,' I shouted, grabbing her and giving her a vigorous shake. Again I saw the look of incomprehension in other people's eyes. She lapsed into allowing her mouth to fill up. The deterioration started and I tried to stem the tide. First I had to turn her face to mine to make her swallow; then I had to bend her head back; and eventually I had to strike her each time her mouth was full. The others sat in embarrassed silence.

'Why don't you just let her spit?' asked John when we reached Sheffield. 'That's what I'd do.'

'But she doesn't want to spit. If I let her spit I'd be letting her down,' I answered, but he was unconvinced.

I was convinced that I had to hold on to Julie and see her through, if she were ever to be the happy out-going child I knew she could be. That day, though, she did not manage to emerge from the depths of her mood.

Towards the end of August there was a new development which, on the face of it, seemed to be just another annoyance, but it would later turn out to be part of the road to recovery. Julie started demanding to go to bed, she wanted to go to bed as soon as she returned home from school each evening. Ever since she had been able to keep her mouth empty there, it had been a place for relaxation and comparative happiness. At first we complied and allowed her to spend the evening in bed. It seemed harmless enough and it did make our lives easier. After a day or two, however, we stopped her going despite her perpetual demands. We felt that she was hiding herself away from the life she had to face. Only later did we use her love of bed in a positive way.

On August 30 we saw that other Julie: the completely relaxed and carefree girl. It was the day that Brian married Jackie. During the morning I took her to the ceremony and, given the circumstances, she behaved quite well. She did moan about the chapel, particularly about it having no steeple, and she did moan about the piano, because she had expected an organ. She did refuse to sit down again after one of the hymns and let out a screech, that turned the heads of the congregation, when I pulled her back down into her seat. She did rush up to Jackie after the ceremony to feel 'baby in tummy', and screamed when Jackie protested that she was not pregnant. That was our fault really. To stop Julie's incessant questioning we had, months before, told her that you had to be married before you could have a baby; and, quite naturally I suppose, she had assumed that Jackie was suddenly pregnant. Yet, throughout it all, she did keep a moderate degree of control and she did manage to swallow each time I squeezed her hand.

It was later that evening at the party that Julie surprised us. We felt that our best plan was to take her to the party, but to leave her upstairs in one of the beds where she would be happy and at least see some of the celebrations.

'What dwinking?' she asked when I went upstairs to see her.

'Beer,' I answered.

'What kind beer?'

'Black beer, I suppose,' I said looking at it.

'Like it,' she said.

'How do you know? You've never had any before.'

'Di',' she said frowning. 'Beer make you dizzy?'

'Yes.'

'Want some. Julie have a swallow.'

'What do you say?'

'Plea'.'

'Well I don't see why not,' I said and allowed her to take a drink.

'Yuer,' she said in disgust. 'Like black beer. More. Plea'.'

'No, not yet.'

'Not dizzy yet,' she said swivelling her head. 'Want more black beer.'

About half an hour later Julie came downstairs into the crowded room. Her face was flushed and her eyes sparkled. Evidently I had not been the only one to visit her with black beer. She was dressed only in purple net tights and a vest: quite a sight at a wedding party. She looked splendidly happy.

'Hello.' I said as she came threading her way towards us. 'Who told you to get up?'

'Nerves,' she said. 'My ner' tell me.' She jumped on to my lap, looked up at me and swallowed. All trace of fear had gone.

'Oh like dat music,' she said to Jade.

'Which music?' asked Jade.

'Oh da ya di di girls, da da di big girl,' she sang in a tuneless voice. 'Oh Jade know. Upstair.'

'You mean that record that was playing when I came to see you upstairs?' asked Jade.

'It i'.'

'Let's go and find it for you then.' They went off hand in hand to the record player. A few minutes later they returned, after changing the record.

'Oh like it. Like it,' said Julie, kicking her legs and waving her arms in a weird dance.

That night guests tickled and played with her and through it all she laughed with a good humour.

'What dat?' she asked.

'Martini,' answered the unsuspecting young lady. Julie grabbed it and downed it before anyone could stop her. She coughed, spluttered and grimaced as if she had been poisoned.

'Like it,' she said. 'Like dis Martini. More plea'.'

Another guest had her fancy platform shoes removed by Julie, though she did ask quite politely before taking them. She clomped round the room, dancing, laughing and drinking, almost the 'life-and-soul' of the party.

When she began to stumble we decided to take her home.

'No, no. Like party. Like it. Like boozing. Do like it now,' she protested, and crumpled up with laughter.

The day after she was as low as ever. All her colour and spirit had drained away. From the moment she woke her eyes read fear and fight. Living with Julie's moods was like riding an emotional roller-coaster.

She was becoming increasingly dissatisfied with her life at home. Her demands were insatiable, particularly her demands to stay with other people and to be taken out. 'Where goin' dis weekend?' was a persistant question. She did spend nights out with Madeline and with Brian, and yet when she returned she was more dissatisfied than ever. Madeline took her to the Isle of Man, and on her return she was extremely nasty in her rejection of us. During the summer months, particularly before the arrival of Anna, we had gone out almost every weekend, but we had become more tied down and also poorer weather was setting in. Julie began to suffer from boredom.

We tried to make her more self-sufficient. She began to go to school unaccompanied in the taxi. Twice she snatched the driver's glasses from his face and was banned to the back seat, but her behaviour improved once she started to 'swallow for taximan'. We sent her on more trips to the post-box at the end of the road. We sent her to the local shop on her own. We sent her, too, to Neil's cottage. It was a ten-minute walk away from our home, but we had often been to visit Neil and his wife Mary, and Julie knew the way well. When that succeeded we tried sending her down to Lumb Bank (the land rented by Neil), which was a twenty-minute walk, promising that we would follow her down five minutes later. This was too far for her. She only managed to get round the corner. There we found her having a tug-of-war with a bemused little old man. She was trying to get him to take her to Lumb Bank, and he was trying to bring her home. The reason for this failure was that Julie knew that it was too far for her to go without swallowing. The length of time she could keep saliva in her mouth was the length of time that she could spend on her own.

The prime barrier to Julie's independence was her mouth. As long as she needed us to make her swallow she was tied to

us and we to her. We were convinced that a whole new world
would open for her if she could stop filling her mouth all the
time and just swallow like everyone else.

Chapter 15

During October and November there were a number of very hopeful changes in Julie's behaviour, but paradoxically these were the very changes which helped precipitate our near loss of Julie.

One evening I took Julie's supper up to her bedroom. It had been one of those fruitless days and her misery had culminated in her being sent to bed early. It was pilchard sandwiches for supper, her favourite snack. I took them upstairs and put them beside her. She looked at them disdainfully.

'I don't care whether you eat them or not,' I said.

'I think it's fish,' she said meaningfully.

'Well, if you think that I'm making you eat your supper after all you've done today, you're wrong,' I said and walked out.

When I went into her room five minutes later she grabbed a sandwich and snatched her first bite of it. I took it from her and headed for the door.

'I told you I wasn't going to make you eat them,' I said.

I expected her to accept this with a pathetic, 'But do like them now', as she had always done previously, but she did not. She came leaping across the bedroom and seized the sandwiches from me.

'I will eat them,' she said. Her positive decisiveness astounded me, and I just left her to it. Within a couple of minutes she had eaten both sandwiches and was down for more. This was the first time she had eaten anything of her own volition since she had been with us; possibly it was the first time in her life.

'Who eat for?' she asked. Her eyes were wide with delight.

'You ate because you wanted to. You ate for yourself, I

suppose,' I answered.

'Eat for Julie,' she said, 'You said it.'

'Eat for Julie,' I said and laughed.

'Adain,' she said.

After that evening she took her supper upstairs every night, and 'ate for Julie'. She was so relaxed that she even crept downstairs and helped herself to biscuits and, on one occasion, a whole box of chocolates to eat in her bedroom.

It was Henry who brought about the next improvement. The relationship between Henry and Julie had grown to friendship. Henry was a friend rather than someone who 'dealt' with her, and she looked forward to him coming home each evening. He began to go to see her in the evenings after she had gone to bed. He would clown with her, pulling the covers off her bed, holding her hands while she bounced on the mattress, and, pretending to be a monster, he would chase her up and down the landing. Through it all, Julie kept her mouth empty: there were no mouthfuls of saliva, and there was no need to tell her when to swallow. Hearing her shrieks of laughter we went upstairs to join in the games. The difference in Julie during those brief periods when we played with her upstairs, after she was supposed to be in bed, was amazing. Her eyes shone with glee. She was as spontaneous and relaxed as when she had been tipsy at Brian's wedding party. There was no nastiness, no moans, no groans, and no fear. We could tickle her and tease her and she would accept it all playfully. The demands were still there, but the disagreeable comments when her demands were not met were gone.

Those specific times, after she had gone to bed, and that specific place, her bedroom, were the kernel from which we started to expand. We left her in the bath to bathe herself. At first, Julie would have a quick dip and rush down to dry herself when her mouth filled with saliva. With some encouragement, however, she began to keep her mouth empty in the bath and then she was able to laze and bath herself at her ease. We began, too, to insist that she did all her own jobs by herself in the morning: this meant going to the toilet, washing, cleaning her teeth and dressing, before she came down for her breakfast. She gradually managed to do

110

all these things without her mouth filling. Over weeks the improvement increased, so that from the time she put on her nightie and went upstairs to bed, until the time she came down for her breakfast she swallowed normally and was a relaxed happy child.

The progress pleased us but it added all the more to our frustration when she regressed. She could go all that time and then, suddenly, after her breakfast, the old problem would start. Her mouth would fill with saliva and she had to be made to swallow. Her attitude, her physical appearance and the look in her eyes would change. Once her mouth was filling with saliva she was the same old Julie, who needed to be forced to swallow. We could not understand why she was unable to swallow on her own. We tried putting her back to bed to begin the day again, but that did not work; whatever we did, however we approached her, nothing worked.

Julie's life at school was ticking over. Neil had left along with Madeline, so we had to rely on Julie's own reports about her life there. She was not eating at school, she was not going to the toilet and she was having to have her nose pressed each time she needed to swallow — this was her regular sparse report. Many evenings she came home in tears, complaining about 'David Hamilton all afternoon', and pleading to be sent to 'new school', but all we could do was to tell her that she had to go to Linwood Side. Time and again we had told her that she was not 'handicap'', but we kept sending her to the 'hospital school'. The contradiction was as apparent to Julie as it was to ourselves.

Towards the end of October Jade's mother came to stay at the cottage for a couple of weeks. We had never quite convinced Jade's mother of the value of fostering Julie. She was sympathetic enough towards her but she saw her as a hopeless case who was not worth all the effort and worry she had caused us. With the birth of Anna matters had come to a head, because she saw Julie as a danger to her grand-daughter. It was easy enough to see why she felt that way but, with her attitude and our desperation for her to see Julie in a good light, relationships were being strained. Julie did not help by being at a miserable low. 'Don't like Mummy,' she said whenever Jade's mother made any of her all too few attempts at talking to Julie. I kept her out of the way as much as I could, by taking her for 'naps' on our bed, and by taking her out some evenings, but I failed to draw her out of her misery. When the baby became ill the atmosphere in the cottage became intolerable.

On the Thursday of the second of those two weeks I came home particularly tired from work to find Julie crouched against the wall and Jade looking pale and sick with worry.

'Anna's no better,' she told me. 'The doctor said that she might have to go to hospital.'

Tea was eaten in an oppressive silence, broken only by Julie's moanings. Afterwards I took what I thought was an easy way out. I took Julie upstairs to lie with me on the bed, where she would keep her mouth empty and we could both relax a little. She crouched there as stiff as a board.

'Who John go to sleep for?' she asked.

'I'm tired, Julie.'

'Why?'

'I'm just very tired. Please let's just be quiet and have a nap, eh?'

'What doing after nap?' she asked. She swallowed as I turned to her.

'Look, Julie, stop it,' I said. 'Why are you waiting for me before you swallow? You like having a nap with me don't you?'

'It i'.'

'We've done it before and you've been all right, haven't you?'

'It i'.'

'Well, please Julie just for half an hour.'

She roused me a couple of times so that I would move and she could swallow as I turned, but I shouted and pleaded with her and she seemed to accept the situation. She cuddled up to me while I went to sleep. As I slept her mouth filled with saliva and her fear grew since she needed some sign to swallow. At other times in that situation she had kept her mouth empty and waited quite happily for me to awake, but that evening she did not. She must have been frozen, watching for the slightest sign to make her swallow, and as I turned in my sleep she jerked away from me and swallowed. I woke and found, not the happy little girl that I had expected to find but, that old stark-white face and those eyes full of terror and hatred. My anger came from the sheer hopelessness and the stupidity of it all.

'Why Julie?' I yelled, hauling her towards me.

'No, no,' she whined, and I hit out at her.

'Just tell me why.'

'No. Will swallow on my own. Will swallow now,' was all she would say, and I hit her again.

'We've given and given and given to you, Julie, and what do you do? Eh? What do you do? You fight us at every turn. You couldn't even give me just half an hour's peace. Why did you have suddenly to start filling your mouth again?' All the disappointments and frustrations of the past weeks and months came flowing out in an emotional outburst.

As Jade came rushing in, I pushed Julie from the bed and she lay on the floor cringing.

'Get your nightie on,' said Jade. Julie backed out of the room and we heard her laughing to herself in her bedroom.

By the time she was ready for bed, it had all passed like an electric storm. She was happy and her mouth was dry.

'Sorry, John,' she said.

'I'm sorry too,' I answered.

She jumped into my arms and we hugged and kissed.

'Sorry, sorry, sorry,' she said.

'All right, Julie. Let's forget about it.'

'Won't do it adain,' she said, and she sounded as if she meant it.

That Friday was, thank goodness, one of Julie's fairly regular visits to see Penny. The break was more than ever welcome. After work I went to the station to meet Jade and Julie, to take Julie to Penny's. She was not there. Jade, and her mother and Anna, were waiting with two social workers, Mr M and his senior, Mr H.

'There's bruising on Julie, and it's been reported,' Jade told me, her voice jerky with anxiety.

It was the beginning of what seemed a nightmare. The social workers took me in their car to collect Julie from school, and as we travelled, I tried to explain the happenings of the previous evening. I listened self-consciously to my own voice. It sounded thin and my reasons very pathetic. The social workers were sympathetic, but quite professional. They used such phrases as: 'With the present climate being as it is . . . .'; 'You can understand our position . . . .'; 'We realize the anxiety this must cause you and your wife'; 'You have our full confidence and backing but . . . .'

By the time we reached the school Julie was in a thunderous mood. It was five o'clock. She had spent a whole hour confined in the headmistress' office being given sips of water every few minutes to keep her swallowing, when she should have been on the train with me.

'Had no tea,' she said in greeting.

'I know,' I answered, and she began her chain of moans and grievances. Somehow, though, it was very reassuring to hear those predictable moans and see the same old Julie.

Mr H handed me a list of the 'areas of bruising on Julie'. The list certainly did look bad and, despite Mr H's conciliatory tone, it felt like being given a charge sheet.

'The bruising was not all done last night,' I heard myself say, 'and some of the bruising was accidental.'

'Can you explain any of the bruises, apart from those caused last night?' he asked.

I could not think. I did not want to think. Everything seemed so confused.

'She bruises very easily, you know,' was all I could say.

Their decision was that, while Julie was staying at Penny's, she would have to be seen by Dr S, who was the head of Community Medicine for their area.

By the time we reached Penny's house I was beginning to brood on the situation, and I half expected Penny to think me a monster. She did not. She began, without hesitation, to defend me and Jade; saying that Julie bruised very easily and comparing her life with us to her life at Rose Hill. It was a relief to hear her talking that way. Julie helped, too, by being the same as ever.

'What for tea?' she asked.

'Egg and chips,' replied Penny.

'Want Jade's tea,' she whined.

Mr M drove me to the station to catch a train back to the cottage.

114

'Do you think she will be returning to us?' I asked him.

He paused for a while.

'I am seventy-five per cent certain that you will have Julie back with you on Monday,' he said.

'And what will happen to her if she doesn't return to us?' I asked.

Again he paused.

'Of that I cannot really say,' he said, 'but I think we would have no option but to return her to Linwood Side.'

On the train back I dwelt on the horror of the situation. We were being seen as people who beat Julie, a defenceless handicapped child, who could be returned to the hospital with another failure on her hands

The time spent in that state of limbo was mercifully short. I rang Mr M on Saturday morning and was told that Julie had already been seen by Dr S. Their decision was that she could return to us, and we could collect her from Penny's on Sunday. There would, however, have to be a meeting, between Jade, myself and the social workers, to discuss the whole matter, and there would have to be no more bruises on her. This meeting was to take place on the following Friday. Before then, though, there were hours of discussion between ourselves and with our friends.

Our friends, in particular Brian and Neil who had known Julie as long as we had, were outraged by our plight. Neil said: 'They don't really care about her. They're just covering themselves. They'd let her go back to that hospital and starve herself. Let them have her at home, even for a day, and then see what they have to say.' They were friends, though, and knew all the details of the situation, and we knew that other people would not be quite so understanding. The whole incident made us reassess our life with Julie. We were failing to make her part of the family; the bruises showed that. We had tried hard, perhaps too hard, and only succeeded in making the situation worse, creating only frustration. On the other hand we knew that Julie had improved and that life with her was getting easier. Above all we knew that we could not bear to lose her. Out of our confusion only one thing seemed obvious: we could not allow it to happen again. We decided that, whenever things were bad, we would put her to bed. If necessary, she would spend the whole day in bed. Though it was not what we wanted for her, and we felt it a cold and almost 'institutional' way of treating her, we could see no alternative.

Present at the meeting were Dr S and Penny, as well as Mr M and Mr H. It took place at our cottage and was more of a informal discussion than an official meeting. Dr S was very understanding. She had known Julie for most of her life, and she seemed delighted with her progress since she had lived with us. She wanted to listen to our problems and offer her help, and her complete lack of condemnation restored our confidence in ourselves. She saw a major problem as being Julie's unhappiness at school. She thought that it was imperative for her to go to a school which more fully met her needs, and promised to do all she could to ensure that she changed schools. It was agreed that, if permission could be obtained, she should be tried at the local primary school.

The incident was to be mentioned again, a number of times, over the months to come, but not always with the sympathetic attitudes shown at that meeting.

Chapter 16

She had not been in bed for longer than an hour before it became intolerable. It was the Sunday following the meeting, and from the first minute of the day, she had been determined to fight us: wanting to be made to do everything. So, keeping to our decision, I had sent her back to bed. She had gone under great protest but since then we had not heard a word from her. Despite my promise I could not help thinking that I was betraying her and ourselves, and my resolve began to fail. I decided to try to compromise.

'OK Julie, get up,' I said, standing at her bedroom door.

'Who get up for?' she asked, emerging from under the covers.

'You're not getting up, you're coming downstairs, and we're going to put you to bed down there.'

'Don't want to.'

'You can sleep on Henry's inflatable mattress. Now wouldn't you like that?'

'It i',' she said without enthusiasm.

'You can bring some covers down if you want.'

'All covers,' she demanded.

We set up her new resting-place behind the settee in the living room. I thought that she would start allowing her mouth to fill with saliva and, within five minutes, I would have to put her back upstairs. She proved me wrong again. She knelt there under the covers, giggling and chattering, without a sign of saliva in her mouth.

'What you doing?' she asked.

'Just sitting here looking at this magazine,' answered Jade.

We had looked after Julie now for about a year and every single day we had had to cope with the same problem: making her swallow every few minutes. The state of Julie's mouth had always dictated any situation. It had never been possible for us to relax with her in the room, because she always seemed so tense and it would become more difficult to keep her swallowing. Now at last, we were sitting in the living room, reading the Sunday papers, and talking to her without worrying about the saliva in her mouth. There was that wonderful new sense of ease and good humour which we had felt during the past few weeks playing upstairs with her.

'Ooo, look at this,' said Jade.

'What? What?' cried Julie.

'It's a picture of a skeleton.'

'I like it. Like it. Canna see it?'

'Yes.'

'Bring it Jade, please,' she said, almost too politely.

'No. You come and get it.'

'Bring it here, please.' There was none of the usual peevishness in her voice.

'You come and get it,' insisted Jade. There was a few seconds wait, and then she jumped out from under the covers.

'Thank you,' she said, taking the magazine from Jade, and she shot back under the covers like a rabbit into its burrow.

Within a few hours she had progressed from needing all her bed-covers, to just needing a sheet and finally to needing no covers at all. She knelt on the mattress fingering through the magazine and talking to us. We did not have to look to see if her cheeks were bulging, and we had no further need to make her swallow. We allowed her to eat her dinner and tea there, and she ate with a healthy appetite and in complete relaxation. The mattress became Julie's refuge and she used it as such whenever we were in the living room.

One of the first changes that the mattress brought was a new-found liking for sweets.

'Canna have another sweetie?' she asked.

'Well you've eaten all those Jade bought for you yesterday, but you can have a chocolate if you want,' I said. It was the following Tuesday evening.

'Yes please,' she said. 'Whole box.'

'No, not the whole box. We want some too, you know.'

She left her mattress to choose her chocolate.

'Do you want that one? It's got a hard centre.'

'Who hard centre for?'

'I don't know. Do you want it or not?'

'Yes. Do,' she said. 'Want two.'

'OK,' I said, and she took them and ran back to her mattress.

She had said everything so naturally that I had not noticed. It was Jade who pointed out to me after she had gone to bed that she had said 'Yes': possibly the first time for many years, certainly the first time since I had known her. It seemed to us that the word 'Yes' symbolized her whole change of outlook. Keeping her mouth empty on the mattress, she was always receptive. She was always ready to play, willing to be tickled or loved, and always open to new suggestions. She had taken the initiative and said 'Yes'.

I suggested that she did some drawing one evening. She had always approached drawing with the same tension with which she approached any task. A piece of paper and a pencil inhibited her. Her drawings had been simple and stereotyped, and drawn to please me rather than herself. Often while drawing she would freeze and wait to be told to continue. The drawings she produced that evening were little different from her previous drawings, but there was a world of difference in her approach. She squatted over them for half an hour,..trying to make them look right, going over lines that were wrong. For the first time she showed a pride in her work.

'Not looking now,' said Julie.

'No, of course you're not,' I reassured her.

'Who not looking for?'

'Because you just keep swallowing now like everyone else.'

'Swallow for Julie,' she said.

'Yes.'

'Why?'

'You just do, don't you?' She hesitated. 'Don't you?' I asked.

'Yes,' she said firmly.

The tables had turned. Suddenly she was not always that careful yard from us; suddenly we were not trying to sever the cords of dependence. She had her 'safe' areas, which were the top storey of the cottage and the mattress, and we were enticing her away from them towards us.

'Watch this,' said Jade, one evening when I had just arrived home from work.

'Spoon game,' she shouted imitating Julie's squeaky voice.

'Spoon game,' came the original squeak, like an echo. Julie was lying upstairs in her usual position, on the landing with her head between the banister rails, waiting for tea and her descent to the mattress.

'Nice one,' squeaked Jade.

'Nice one,' came the echo.

'Good chemicals.'

'Good chemicals.'

'Like it.'

'Like it,' said Julie who had crept down to the kitchen doorway. Jade dipped the ladle into the stew and pulled out a piece of turnip. She handed the ladle to Julie who bounded back upstairs with her prize.

'She'll eat anything like that,' Jade told me. 'Half-cooked potatoes, anything.' Seconds later Julie was back again with an empty ladle and an empty mouth. Her face was full of cheek and impudence.

'Adain,' she said and was gone.

Slowly her 'safe' area crept towards the kitchen. A week later I came home to find Julie sitting on the bottom step yelling: 'Spoon game', 'Nice one', 'I like it', 'Yes please'. I no longer came home to tears, exasperation and coldness. These were giving way to happiness and laughter. The 'safe' area of the mattress also began to spread. She would only have to take a step towards it, or sometimes just look at it, before she would swallow.

Her interest in Anna grew and with it came a renewal of interest in her past life.

'Anna a girl?' Julie asked whilst helping Jade to change her nappy.

'Of course she is,' Jade answered.

'Julie a girl?'

'Of course you are.'

'Want boy. Boy better,' she said frowning. 'Canna be a boy?'

120

'Don't be silly.'

'Who can't be boy for?'

'Because you're a girl.'

'Oh, born dat way.' She paused. 'Julie spitting when baby?' she asked.

'No,' said Jade laughing.

'Who Julie spit for?'

'Why did you spit, Julie?'

'Oh, at Rose Hill. Spitting at Rose Hill.'

'Why did you spit at Rose Hill?'

'Unhappy dere. Dat why.'

She still spoke without emotion about her past, but, in those weeks before Christmas, there was a new understanding in what she had to say.

'Anna, Anna,' she squealed. Julie was laying on her mattress, and I was bouncing Anna on it. 'Anna not going to Coventry Hou' School?' she asked.

'Were there babies at Coventry House?' I asked.

'Oh, yes. Coventry Hou' School babies.'

'Well, Anna won't be going there.'

'Julie be baby like dat?' she asked.

'What do you mean? You want to be a baby like Anna?'

'It i',' she answered.

'What do you want to be like Anna for?' I asked wondering if it was the first signs of jealousy.

'Oh, Anna not going to Coventry Hou' School first time,' she answered.

Julie began to take a delight in making us laugh. She became quite a clown.

'Hello wall. How are you wall?' she said grinning.

'What's wrong with you?' I asked her laughing at her.

'Oh, talking to wall. Dat's funny.' She creased with laughter and rolled off her mattress.

'You're silly,' I said.

A minute later I heard a cheeky voice whisper: 'Hello wall. Hello my darling.'

Our friends saw and understood. They rejoiced with us. Jade took Julie to visit Neil and Mary. Julie danced into their house. She burrowed under Mary's jumper; 'Mary having baby. I'll be Mary's baby,' she announced. She ran up and

121

down their stairs playing with their three children; and there was no saliva in her mouth. She chattered and joked with Mary and Neil; and there was no saliva in her mouth. They said that she looked a different child without her cheeks bulging with saliva. Penny, of course, was overjoyed. The circumstances of a visit by Julie to her just before Christmas were a happy contrast to the circumstances of her previous visit.

Changes were coming for her in her school life, which was just as well, as she had become desperately unhappy at Linwood Side. She was still filling her mouth with saliva there, and they were still having to press her nose to make her swallow. The threat of Monday morning and 'hospital school' never failed to depress her each Sunday evening. 'Not handicap' now,' she kept saying. There were plans afoot to terminate her placement at Linwood Side School, and to try her, on an experimental, part-time basis, at the local primary school.

We spent the Christmas of 1975 at my parents' home that year. Julie was good, though she did view the world as her oyster, and felt that she should be given all the riches she desired since she was keeping her mouth empty. She would not accept 'No' for an answer, and flew into a rage whenever her desires were frustrated.

'No. Sorry, Julie, there just aren't any pilchards in the house,' my mother explained for the third time in response to Julie's demands of 'Pilchards for supper.' It was the evening of our arrival.

'But do keep swallowing,' said Julie.

'It's nothing to do with that,' I told her.

'You'll have to make do with sardines tonight, I'm afraid,' said my mother.

'Want pilchards,' she screeched.

Most of the exchanges between my parents and Julie were far happier, however. There were no comments about 'iceberg', and no demands that my father should cross his legs.

'What on earth's that?' asked my mother.

'Monkey,' answered Julie. The monkey in question was a two foot stuffed toy. 'Thank you, Mummy,' she said after a

122

prompting nudge.

'She bought it with that money you gave us to get her a Christmas box,' I explained.

'You're welcome,' said my mother. 'It's a beauty. What are you going to call it?'

'Tiny,' answered Julie. 'Oh, Tiny in hospital,' she reminded my mother, who knew nothing of Tiny.

'Where did you get it from?'

'Let's pretend in shop,' said Julie, handing the monkey to my mother. 'Oh monkey! Monkey!' she shrieked, jumping for joy. 'Rubber hands! Rubber feet! Rubber head!'

'You did that in the shop?' asked my mother.

'It i',' said Julie.

'She did,' confirmed Jade, 'except about ten times louder than that.'

'Where Tiny now?' Julie asked me, suddenly frowning.

We allowed her to eat her meals on the stairs. My parents were a little surprised at this arrangement, but it pleased her and our meals could be eaten in peace. She ate plenty of food in complete relaxation, and she could thrust her head into the dining room to make the odd comment, or to show us Tiny whose feet she kept polishing with bread and butter.

'Dind-a-ling,' shouted Julie. It was Christmas Eve afternoon.

'Pardon?' I said.

'I'll be Santa Claus,' she said. 'Wait a minute. Wait a minute.' She jumped up from the settee, where I had been trying fruitlessly to persuade her quietly to watch television, and ran from the room.

'Dind-a-ling. Dind-a-ling,' she shouted through the closed door, then in she crept with an invisible sack on her back.

'Close eyes. Close eyes,' she ordered and I obeyed. 'Dind-a-ling. You be Julie, all right?'

'All right,' I answered

'Dere,' she said, placing an invisible parcel in my lap. I ceremoniously unwrapped it, going through all the motions of surprise and pleasure.

'Oh, that's lovely,' I said 'Thank you very much Santa Claus.'

'No, no,' she yelled. 'Don't like it. Don't want it,' she

whined, scowling and giving an all too recognizable imitation of herself.

When it came to the real opening of presents the next morning, the real scowl was seen and the real whine was heard, but it only lasted while she opened her first present. Soon there was the smile. 'Like dis. What dis?' she said, giving each parcel a good pummel and shake. 'Feel heart. Who heart beating fast for?'

Julie added to the pleasure of Christmas, rather than almost ruining it as she had the previous year.

Chapter 17

After Christmas we had a six-week waiting period before we went away. I had resigned from my teaching post and we had some free time on our hands. An opportunity had arisen for us to stay on an island off the Scottish coast for a while and we had taken it with both hands. Our flight was booked for mid-February.

Those six weeks were quite a new situation for Julie. She was no longer attending Linwood Side School, and we were waiting for a decision to be made about her attendance at the local primary school: so she was at home in the cottage all day. We thought that it would have been a happy situation, especially with my being home all day, but we were wrong. Once again Julie regressed. Even the mattress lost its magical powers and her mouth began filling with saliva again. The happy child was gone, and we mourned her loss. Tension crept into our cottage again, but we had come to know it and its dangers. We knew how to handle the tension and we also knew that Julie would come through again. We did not allow her to stay in her depression, nor did we allow her to pull us down into it. We treated her much the same as we had always done and, after two weeks, she began to rise again. The scowl and hunched shoulders went, and the ready smile was back for all to see.

We had been home for two weeks when we had a visit from an education welfare officer. It was Jade who answered the door.

'I'd like to see Julie Lincoln,' he told her stepping into the cottage and heading for the kitchen.

'She isn't in there,' said Jade, recognizing him but wondering why he should want to see Julie. 'She's in the bedroom.'

Once in the bedroom he seemed to become hesitant and embarrassed. 'Good morning, Julie,' he said, peering at her.

'Good morning. What your name?' she asked smiling at him. She was having a 'lie in' in our bed that morning for being good, and was in quite a happy mood.

That was the end of the conversation. He wanted no more from Julie. He followed Jade downstairs, and asked us why she had not been to Linwood Side School for two weeks. We explained the situation while he jotted down a few notes in his note-book, and then he left us to ponder over his peculiar visit. What state had he expected to find Julie in? Evidently the happenings of early November were still fresh in some people's minds.

Julie was eventually allowed to go to the local primary school, after a head of special education, an educational psychologist, the education welfare officer, the social workers and the headmistress had all aired their views, compromised and recompromised. She was allowed to go for two afternoons a week, and only then on the basis of visiting, and she had to be accompanied by either myself or Jade. We managed to have five such visits before going to Scotland.

Julie behaved well during those visits, for Julie that is, keeping a veneer of self-control which only occasionally broke into screeches. There were a few minor misdeeds, such as using too much paint and insisting on slapping her hands in it, and there was an incident which occurred when the teacher was reading to the class. Julie suddenly leapt from her seat and grabbed the book from the teacher. 'Too long. Don't like dis book,' she said, flicking through the pages. The book was set in London at the turn of the century and its hero happened to be a deprived orphan. If I had not intervened the teacher would have had to fight to get her book back. She did nothing drastically wrong. She did not kick, swear, point at her crutch, fill her mouth with saliva, or do any of the various things she could have chosen from her repertoire of unacceptable behaviours, yet Julie never looked at home in the school.

The initial joy of seeing her bouncing aboard her space-hopper into a class of walking, talking, normal children soon dissipated and was replaced by a deep sadness for her. She was so near and yet so far away. With her Chaplinesque walk, long-fingered wild gestures and high-pitched excited voice she was a compelling child, and she attracted the other children to her. Yet the contact between herself and the other children was, as the headmistress said, very 'one-sided'. Julie was only interested as long as they obeyed her and played her 'leg-crossing game'. She showed no interest in joining in their activities and their games. The words 'Don't like dis girl' slipped so easily and thoughtlessly from her tongue and, try as I might to repair the damage, 'dis girl' retired hurt and would not approach so enthusiastically again. It was evident that Julie was just as isolated and out of place in that class as she had been in her class at Linwood Side School.

She was a total stranger to all the unwritten rules and self-discipline that being in a primary school involve. To have to sit for two minutes in silence had Julie on the edge of a tantrum. Her behaviour was similar in a number of ways to that of children in a nursery or reception class, but, at thirteen she was too old to be allowed to start right at the beginning. The headmistress summed up the 'experiment' quite fairly by saying that she was 'pleasantly surprised' by Julie's behaviour, but that they could not have coped with her unaccompanied by Jade or myself.

'Did you break that tooth?' I asked Julie one evening. She had a fine set of slightly prominent teeth which she looked after meticulously, brushing them morning and night without fail. Along the lower set there was one broken tooth.

'Break tooth,' she said with a laugh, feeling the tooth in question. 'Daisy.'

'Who's Daisy?' I asked.

'Wouldn't wee for Daisy.'

'What happened?'

'Oh, jug.'

'A jug?'

'Pour water. Help to wee.'

'Where did she pour the water?'

'All over,' she said, running her hands over her body.

'And how did that break your tooth?'

'Oh, jug,' she said, demonstrating how the jug had hit her in the mouth.

'Did you wee in the end?'

'No,' she said. 'Don't like Daisy.'

'Where did you know Daisy?'

'Rose Hill,' she said. 'Canna see it? Visit hostel?'

'No, but we're going to Coventry House and to see Miss Campbell soon, like I promised.'

At the beginning of February, when Julie was outward and receptive again, I took her on that long promised trip: the trip to see Coventry House School, and the children's home which she had once lived in. We went first to Coventry House, having first gained the permission of the headmistress there.

'Can smell Coventry House air,' she said as we entered the school. 'Poo stinks.' The smell was familiar. If I had closed my eyes, my ears and nose would have told me that I was on C ward.

Julie careered around the classrooms in wild excitement, and as she went she painted the picture of her past life: pointing out the chair she had refused to sit in; inspecting the floor where she used to stand; showing me the toilet which she would not use. She showed great interest in the children, and, as usual, she preferred the most severely physically and mentally handicapped children. One boy, of about five, who lay on his back with his legs stiff in the air, engrossed her for a while. 'Who can't walk for?' she asked. 'Heels doing down?' 'Legs in air all time?'

Many members of the staff had moved on since her time there. Some remembered her, though, but Julie showed no affection towards them and they showed little for her.

'Hello, Julie,' said one rather tall stately lady. 'Remember me?'

'What your name?' she asked.

'Oh surely you remember me,' said the lady.

Julie paused and frowned, and then the light dawned: 'Oh I remember. Fish,' she said. 'Wouldn't eat fish.'

The lady turned away and Julie continued her exploration. I resisted the temptation of asking what had happened when she had refused to eat the fish.

'So you don't spit now,' said another of the teachers.

'Keeps swallowing,' answered Julie.

'And you've decided to keep your clothes on I see.'

She did not answer. She was too busy hauling a boy on to his feet to see if he could walk. The teacher turned to me.

'The last I can remember of her, she wouldn't wear a stitch of clothing. Everything we put on her, she just ripped it off.'

At four o'clock we caught a bus down the road to the children's home, following the route that she had travelled so many times by ambulance. Julie hammered on the door and it was answered by Miss Campbell, who was expecting us.

'Just a minute. Just a minute,' said Julie, removing her hat and coat and hanging them on a hook in a row of coat-hooks in the hall. She then leapt into Miss Campbell's arms. Julie had come home.

'It's nice to see you,' said Miss Campbell. She looked in amazement at the girl in her arms.

From behind Miss Campbell emerged a girl of about Julie's age, shyly smiling. Julie slipped from Miss Campbell's arms and the girl took her hand.

'Canna play with Jenny?' asked Julie but before anyone could answer she had dashed off into the dining room.

'Oh dere it i'. Dere it i',' she cried joyfully. She had knelt on the floor and was studying the lino.

'There's what?' I asked her.

'It's her little mark,' said Miss Campbell. 'She used to go on and on about that mark.'

I saw what they meant. It was a small indentation in the lino, no wider than a quarter of an inch and barely visible.

'Used to stand here,' said Julie having jumped to her feet and positioned herself with her back to the wall. 'Oh look! Can still see it.'

'That was one of her places.' Miss Campbell told me. 'She used to stand there, or by the radiator here.'

'No, not dere. Just here,' said Julie showing us the exact spot.

'Yes, that's right, dear,' said Miss Campbell. 'She just wouldn't move,' she told me.

'Go upstairs with Jenny?' asked Julie.

'If it's all right with Miss Campbell,' I answered.

'Of course,' said Miss Campbell, and the two girls ran off hand in hand. 'Jenny and Julie came here at about the same time. They grew up like sisters. She still talks of Julie quite often.'

While they were gone Miss Campbell talked to me about Julie's decline. She told me how her 'quirks' had developed and she had had to be moved to Rose Hill. She spoke quietly, with obvious feeling for Julie.

'Like it. Like spacehopper. Canna have it? Take it home?' Julie came bouncing back on a large orange spacehopper, squealing with delight.

'No, love. It's not yours,' I said.

'It i'. Yes it i',' said Julie indignantly, looking to Miss Campbell for confirmation.

'Yes it probably was hers,' said Miss Campbell 'She can have it if she wants. We've plenty of others.'

'Did she have many toys?' I asked, 'because she didn't bring any to the hospital.'

'Didn't she? She left here with a load of toys,' said Miss Campbell in surprise. 'She didn't play with any of them any more, though,' she added quietly.

Julie dragged me away to show me her old home. She bounced along from room to room with Jenny and myself following. Her face beamed all the while. There was no trace of regret in her voice when she asked 'Who sleep in Julie's bed now?' or when she said 'Where Julie's shoes?' as she rummaged through the shoe cupboard. Even when she showed me the step where she used to kneel, masturbating and spitting, watching the other children playing on the lawn, her eyes still shone.

'Oh, I remember,' said Julie as a parting comment to Miss Campbell, 'use pin. Oh, pin on toilet.'

'Say good-bye properly,' I told her.

'Good-bye,' said Julie.

'Good-bye,' said Miss Campbell and Jennifer.

As she bounced on her spacehopper down the path in front of me I felt proud to be with such a brave girl. She could go back and face her past with open eyes and laughter, and I knew that I had been privileged to see it and to be there with her. I had helped her, Jade had helped her, but in the end the effort had come from Julie. I wondered at the strength of will in that frail child. She had closed herself with

130

a will of steel and what a power of strength it had taken to reopen herself.

'What was that about a pin?' I asked when we had rounded the corner.

'Oh, pin to scratch iceberg out,' she answered, giving me an all too vivid mime.

On February 16, a damp drizzly evening, Henry drove us to the station. We faced a twelve-hour journey, through the night, to Scotland. Julie was apprehensive, not of leaving the house she knew nor of leaving the people she knew, but of where and how she would brush her teeth that night. She had seen her bed stripped during the day and her linen stored away, but she showed no fear. She knew that she could place some trust in us. We were going away as a family. Julie had been with us for eighteen months.

Conclusion

We took Julie into the warmth of a family and she fought us tooth and nail; she knew no other way. We held her in the family and made her take the distasteful medicine. We could not, and did not, accept her as a handicapped child who could not cope with life. We gave her all the intense personal care and attention she so craved, and which she had missed in her early years, but we expected her to give, and, at first, made her give, in return. We berated and praised, slapped and kissed her. We poured the whole range of human emotions over her. Even when she was away or asleep, we did little else but talk about her: her problems and her progress. We ate, slept, and breathed Julie.

In many ways we have succeeded. Julie is still with us, and we are still coping. She has grown to be fit and healthy, active and happy. She sees a life beyond herself, her mouth, her bowels, her bladder, beyond the floor, and beyond shoes. She is outward, inquisitive, spontaneous, mischievous, and, sometimes, giving. She says 'Yes'. Yet we could never fully compensate for those first eleven years of her life. All her old problems still lurk in the background ready to engulf her whenever she hesitates. They can come like a wave from nowhere and for no reason, and, if we do not stem the tide, she is lost. In times of stress she will not face the difficulty with new-found strength or by turning to myself or Jade; she will close all the doors and transform herself into the 'handicapped' child. If she returns to institutional care and the care is impersonal, she will undoubtedly regress to the child she was, and possibly to a worse state.

We have learnt many lessons the hard way. We learnt never to reject or isolate her, never to suggest, directly or indirectly, that her being with us depended on her behaviour.

We learnt how to control our emotions, and how to remain detached without withdrawing in any way. This was the 'professionalism' that we needed to survive the regressions and swings in mood. We found we needed the help of others to ease the tension in our home. Penny, in particular, helped by relieving us of Julie for an occasional weekend. Without Penny we could not have continued.

There is, as yet, little hope for Julie's future. We have still to find a school which will cope with her and also meet her needs. There was an attempt to school her while we were in Scotland. She was collected one morning by a tall, smart educational psychologist who took her to be 'tried' at the local school for mentally handicapped children. She screamed, swore like a trooper and had to be dragged from the car. They returned three quarters of an hour later. Julie pulled the reluctant man to his car. His hair was bedraggled and his air of professional confidence had been severely tried. He declared Julie to be maladjusted and not, definitely not, mentally subnormal, although he could not think of any school for the maladjusted that would accept her. Since then we have returned to our cottage in the north of England and I have been acting as 'home tutor'. This arrangement is far from satisfactory but, as yet, no alternative has proved to be practical.

New problems are developing. Anna is now an active toddler who explores her world with a will and our energy and resources are usually stretched to the limit. Jade is expecting another baby and we just do not know how long we shall be able to cope with Julie at home all the time. The social services will give us no assurances about her placement if we can no longer care for her and there is little doubt that in those circumstances she would return to Linwood Side Hospital.

At the moment we are content. We tolerate Julie when she is in misery and appreciate the times of relative tranquillity when her joy is contagious. We know that it has been worth the cost of the strain on the family and we are determined to cope with her as long as we possibly can.

133

Julie is one of many children who suffer from 'maternal deprivation' and 'institutionalization'. These are children who, for one reason or another, have been deprived of an upbringing in a family from an early age, and have not managed to develop the emotional self-sufficiency to relate to other people. They are cold children. Often they disrupt the normal running of institutions and they descend the rocky road to impersonal care. Julie went from a children's home to a hostel, to a hospital; other children go from a children's home to a community school, to prison; from one institutional 'home' to the next, and with each move their difficulties are compounded. Treatment, and care itself, is defied by the child until it is almost abandoned and the condition accepted. Fostering can be the best form of treatment for such children, providing for them the very thing they have been deprived of.

Fostering is, under the present system, done on a strangely indefinite basis: by voluntary, unpaid, untrained members of the community. At all times the social worker, and his seniors, are legally responsible for the child's welfare. The child can be removed from the foster family at a moment's notice, and the foster parents can hand the child back in the same way. The fostering of such disturbed children as Julie is rare under the present system, and even when it does happen the probability of failure is known to be high. Once a child has been in institutions for over three years his ability to fit into family life can be seriously impaired. Julie had been in institutions for nine years and, for obvious reasons, she was not on any fostering list. The system works well for less disturbed children and short-term cases, but fostering children who need such intense long-term care and personal commitment as Julie is not compatible with the traditional non-professional role of a foster parent.

The answer is to have fostering of disturbed children, and also mentally handicapped children, on a professional basis, as a form of treatment ranking along side other forms of treatment. A number of authorities are already experimenting with small pools of trained professional foster parents. With schemes such as these, children like Julie will have more chance of being fostered. The possibility of fostering will not rely just on circumstances, as it did with Julie. Professional foster parents will be able to help many children who, because they would be too much of a strain within a normal foster home, would otherwise have spent the rest of their lives within institutions.

There is a danger in this system, however, in that a professional foster home could degenerate only too easily into a mini institution. The basic dilemma is that fostering can never really be a job. How can people be paid for accepting a child into their family and for looking after the child as if it were their own? There can be no working hours, no demarcation of duties, and it is difficult to see how there can be holidays. I cannot see that the problem is insuperable though, and the answer probably lies in keeping the foster parents very much as free agents. The social services could contract a professional foster family to look after a long-term foster child for at least a year, with statutory conditions for breaking the contract by either side. Statutory six monthly medical examinations and six monthly reviews would cover both sides.

As to the cost of keeping children in various forms of care I can say a little. Though I have not the exact figures, I know that the cost of keeping Julie in the hospital was over £30 a week and if we add to that the cost of the 'special diet', Julie must have been costing the authority at least £50 a week. The cost of keeping children in more specialized institutions with higher staff ratios is even higher. I have worked in an institution which was costing the authority over £100 per week for each of the twenty children within the institution. We are paid a supplement above the normal rate for fostering (to pay for damage to property done by Julie), but still we are given less than £10 a week to pay for Julie's keep, with quarterly clothing allowances of about £25. So, as well as the benefit to the child, a scheme of professional fostering must, in the long run, save money for the authority.

Fostering will not cure every child's ills. It is questionable whether children who have suffered as badly as Julie can be 'cured'. Yet fostering can ease their pain and treat some of their more obvious wounds, and every child who is being kept within an institution should be considered for fostering.

135

It was early spring. The sun was high and the sky cloudless. We were walking down a long deserted road, going to the sea.

'Too hot for me,' said Julie. 'Canna take jumper off?'

'All right,' said Jade.

'Canna take vest off?' said Julie as she stripped to her waist.

'Since you've done it already, I suppose you can.' She mounted her spacehopper and bounced ahead of us down the road.

'Look, Julie,' said Jade, 'in that field.'

'It's the sea,' she cried.

'No, we're not at the sea yet. I meant that white horse over there,' said Jade.

'Oh, thought was sea,' said Julie with a disappointed frown.

'White horse, white horse bring me good luck,' I said and spat.

'Urgh. Who spit for?' said Julie in disgust.

'That's what you do when you see a white horse,' I said. 'You say: White horse, white horse bring me good luck, and you spit once for luck.'

'Get away with you,' said Jade.

'No, it is, really. My mum told me that.'

'Never heard of that before,' said Jade.

'You mucky thing,' said Julie, 'You be Julie. I'll be John. OK?'

'All right,' I said, laughing.

'You naughty girl,' she said seriously wagging her finger at me. 'You been spitting, haven't you?' It was such a good impersonation that Jade and I could not help but laugh. Suddenly her face clouded into a scowl: 'Too cold for me,' she whined.